ROSETTES

Scroll Saw Patterns

Marcus Clemons

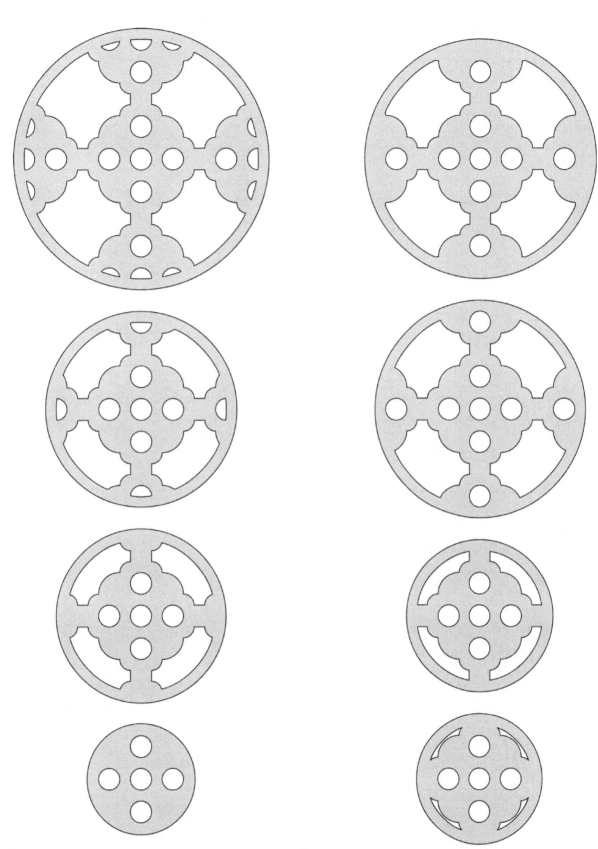

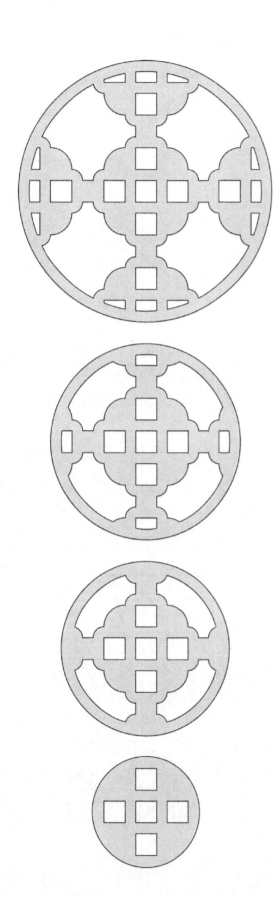

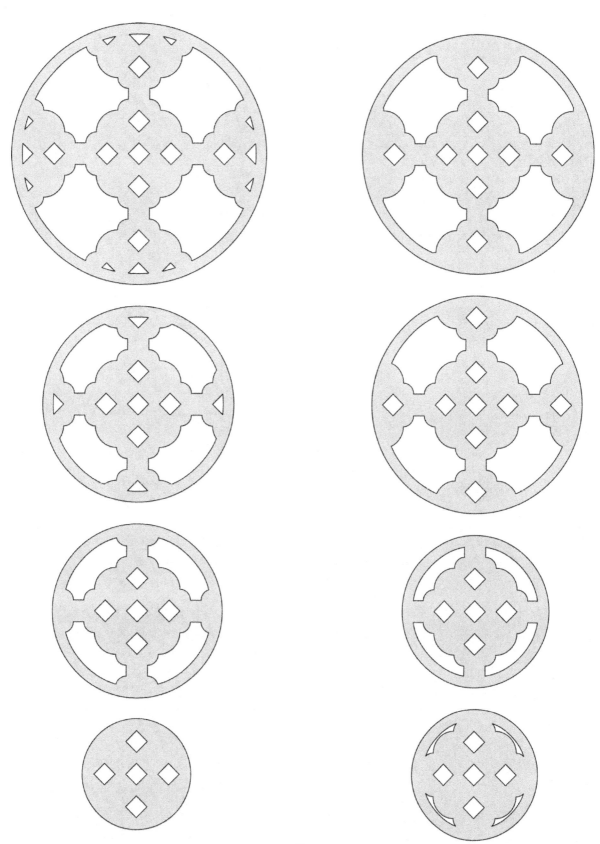

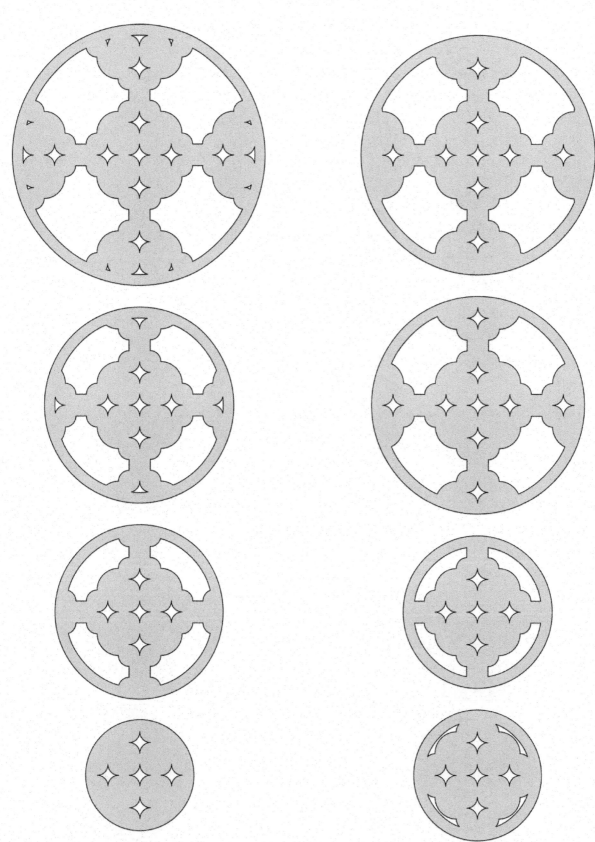

8

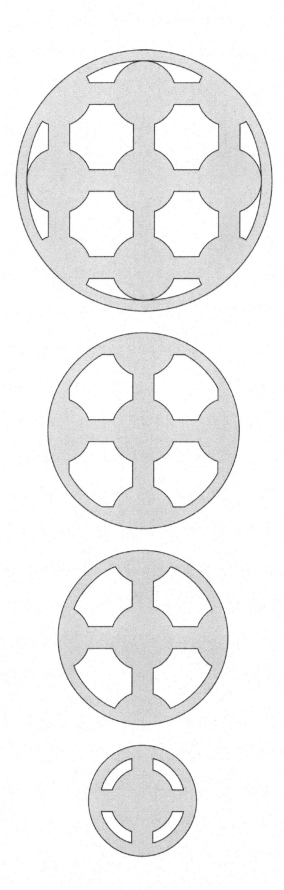
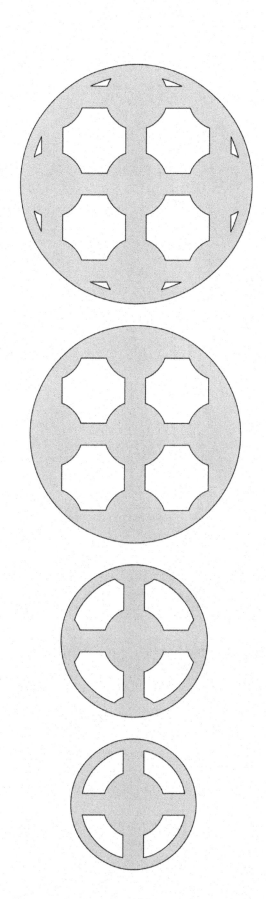

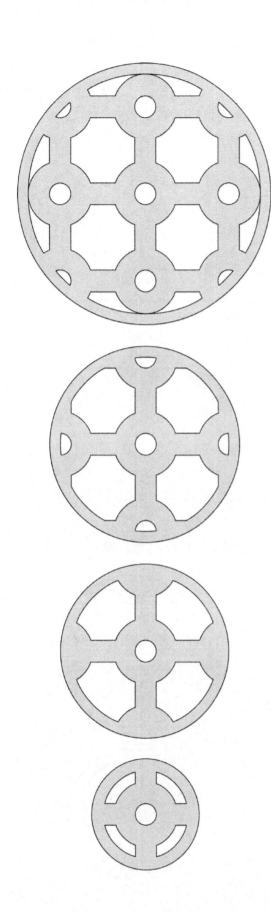
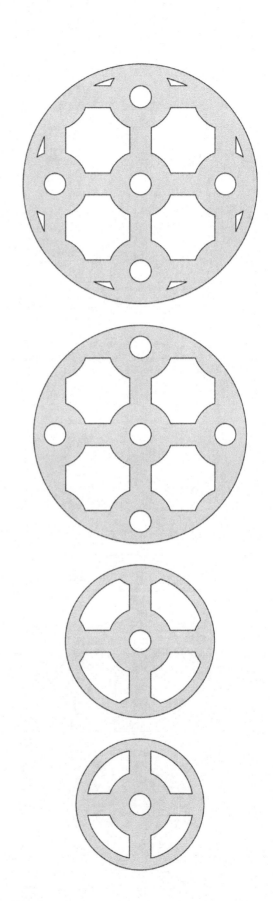

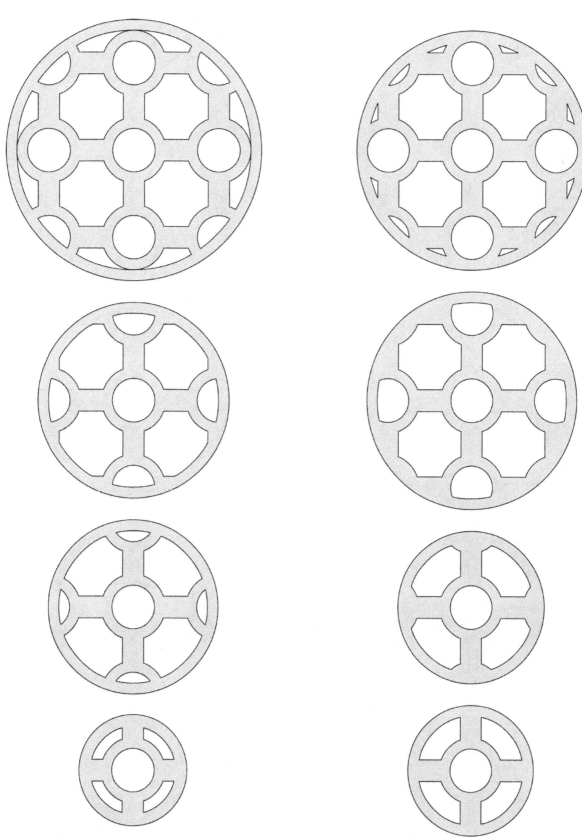

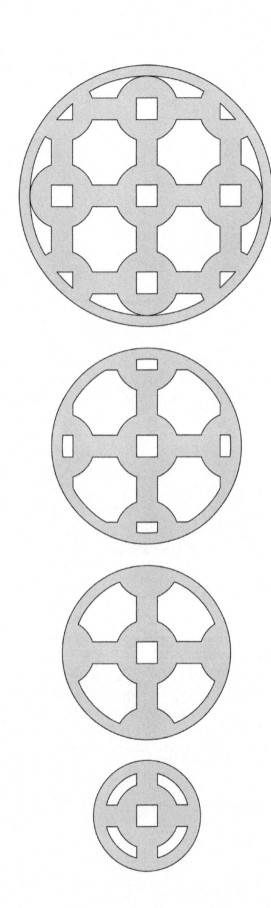
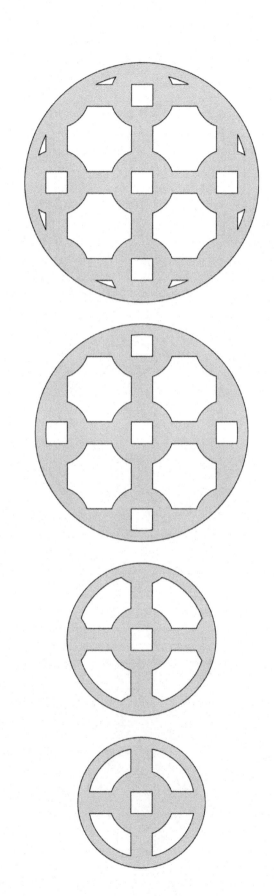

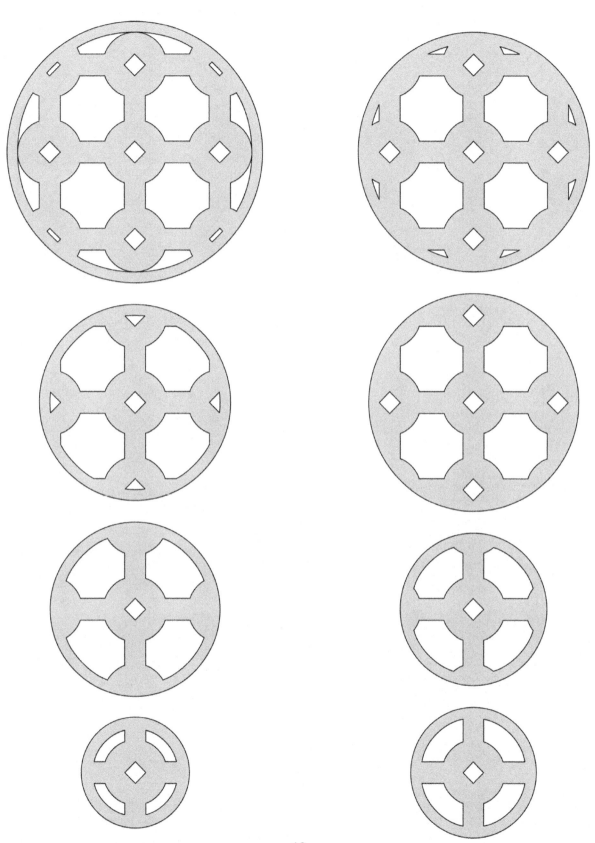

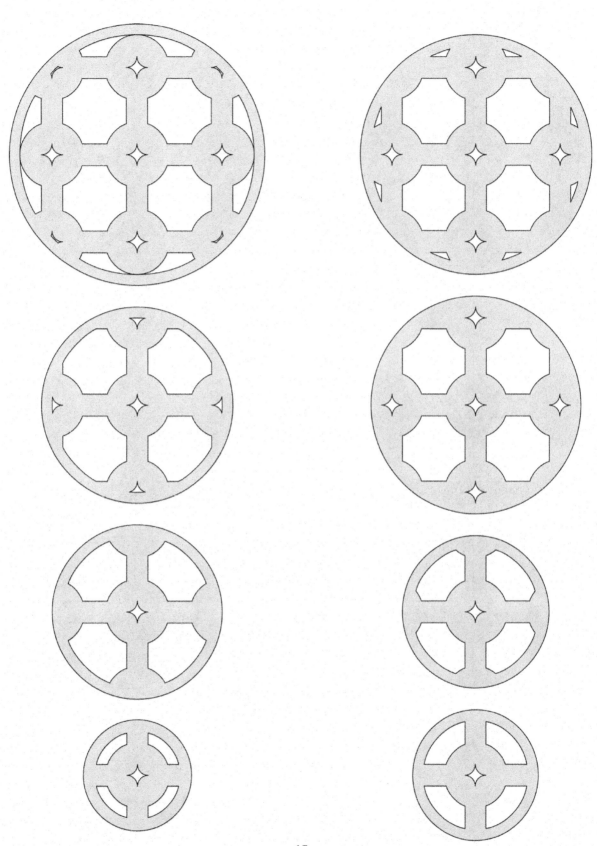

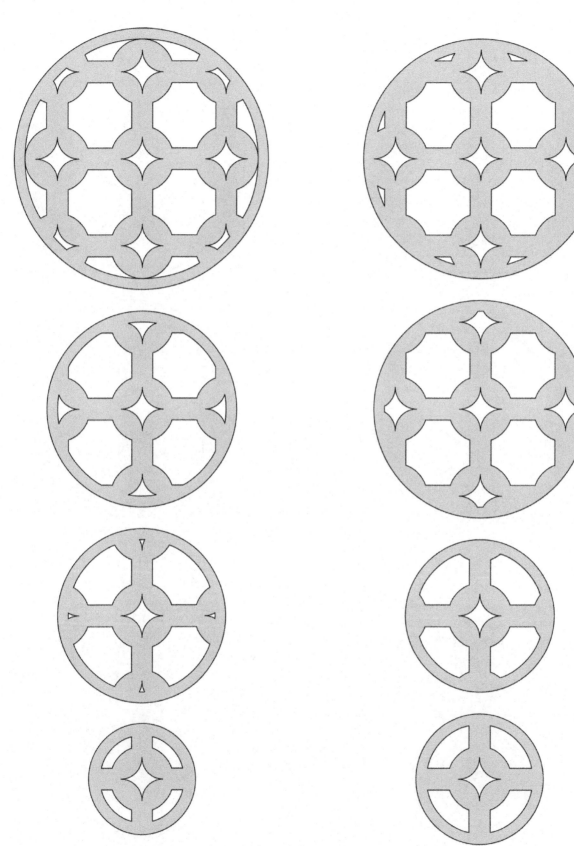

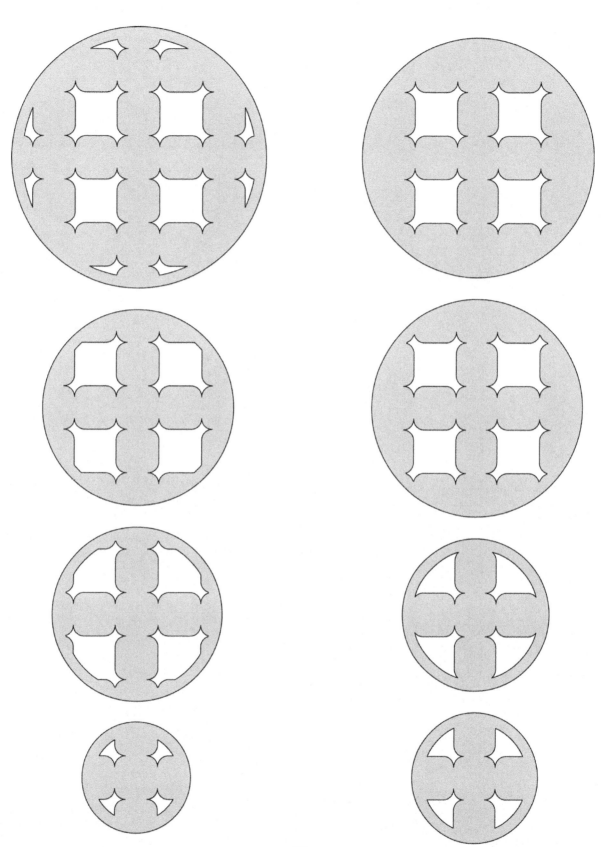

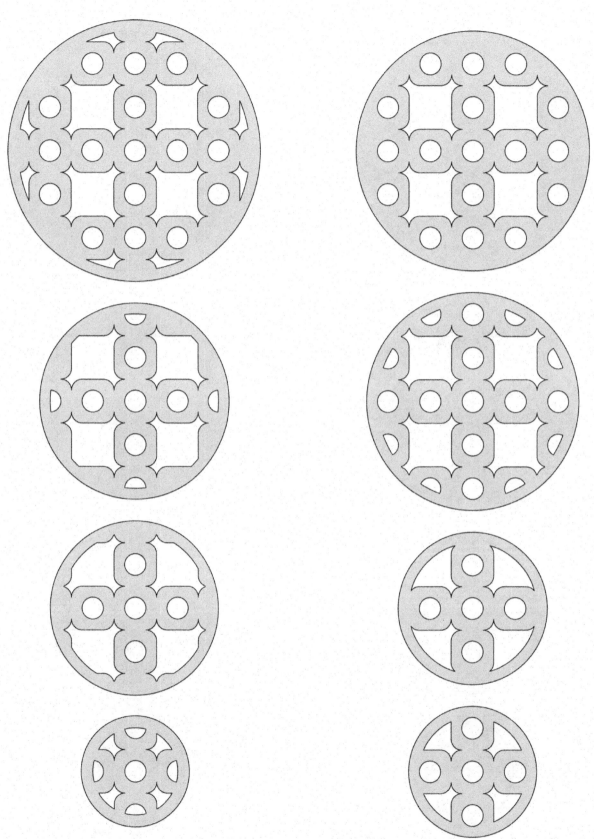

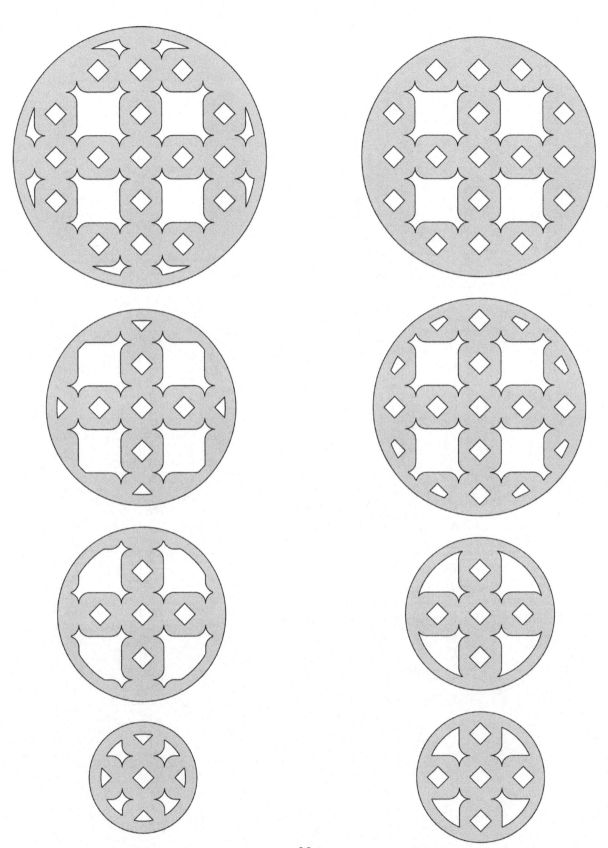

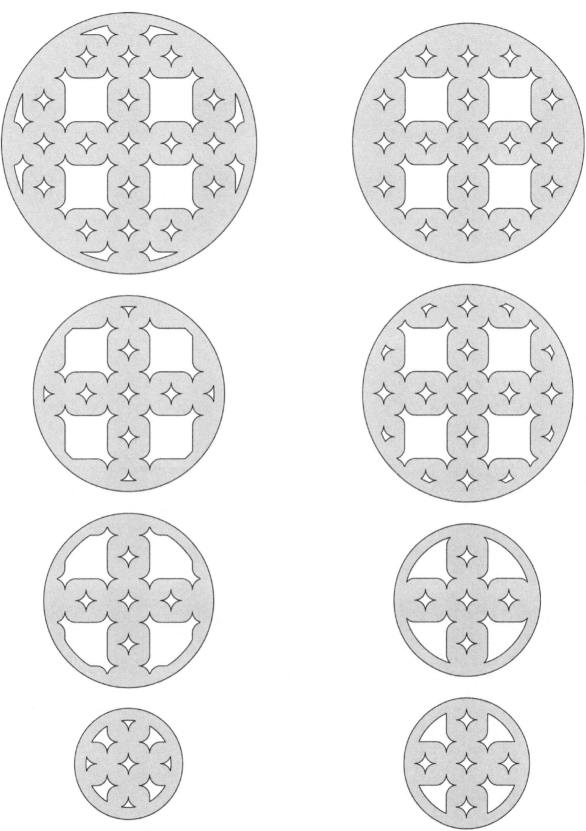

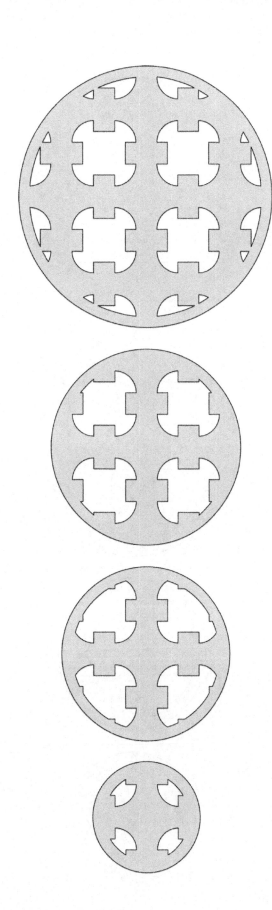

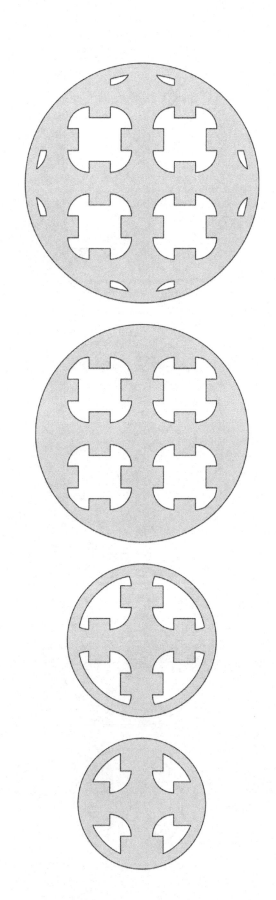

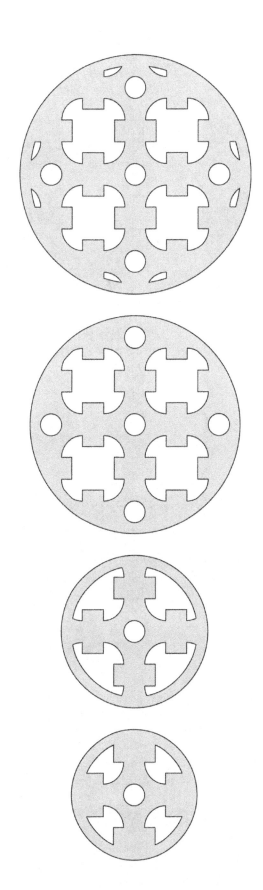

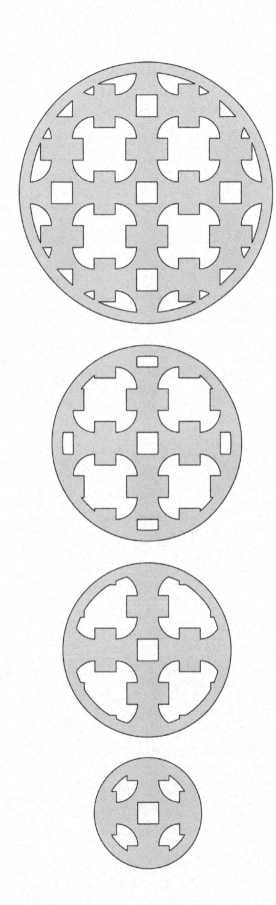
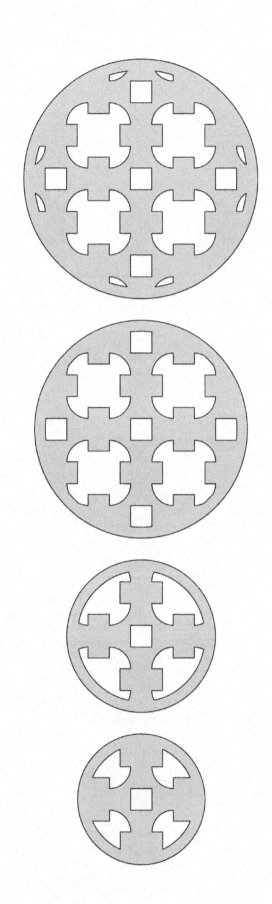

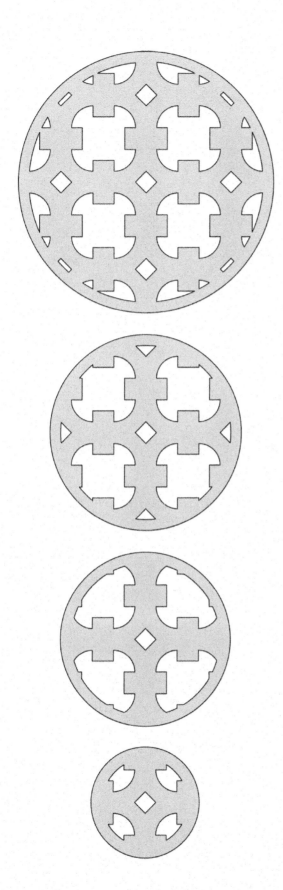
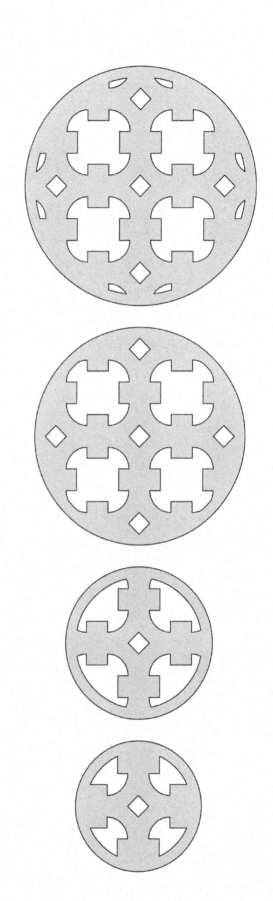

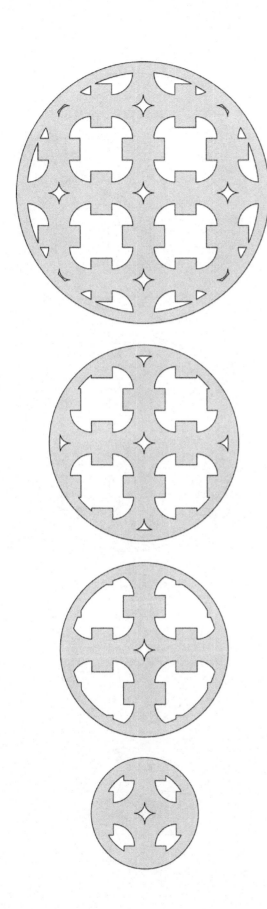
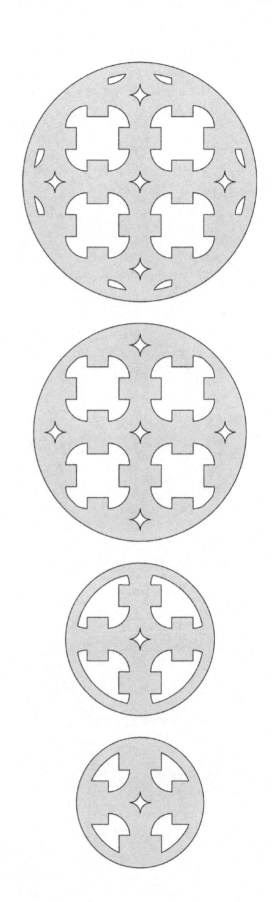

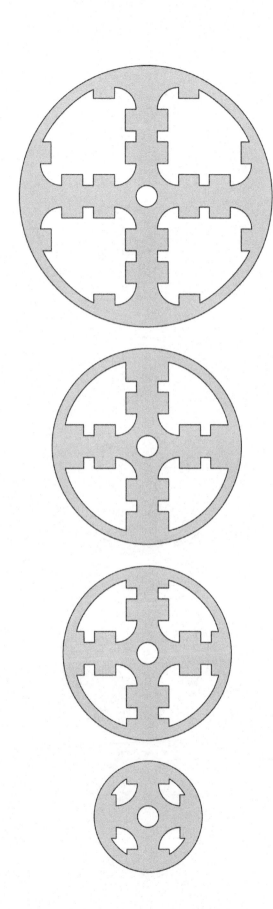

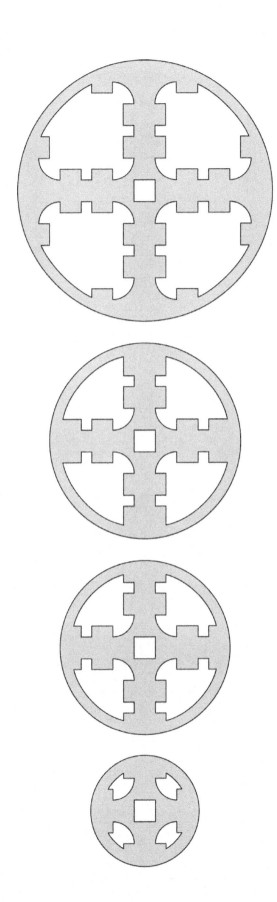

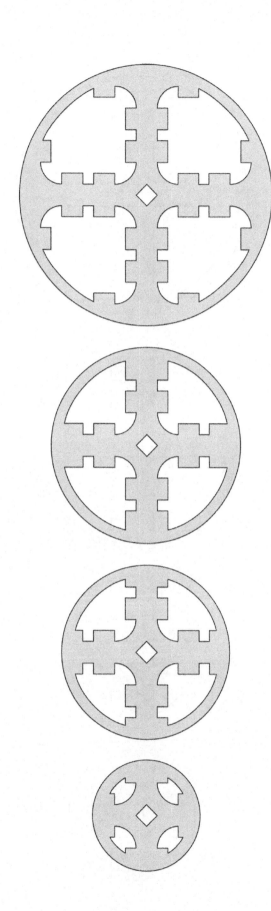

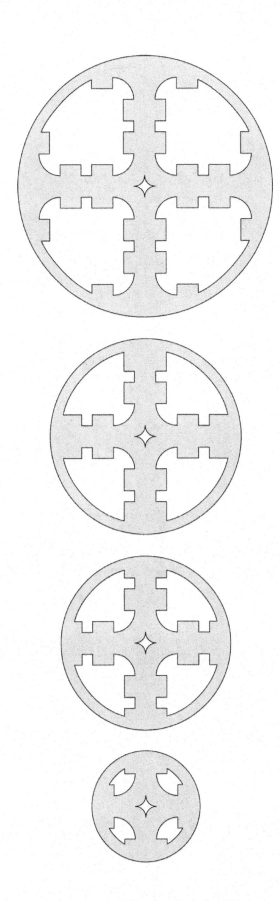
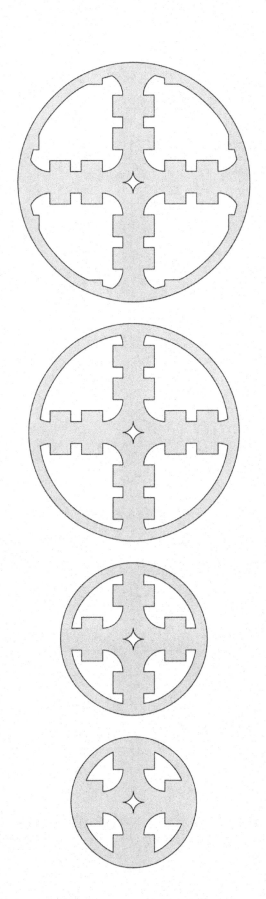

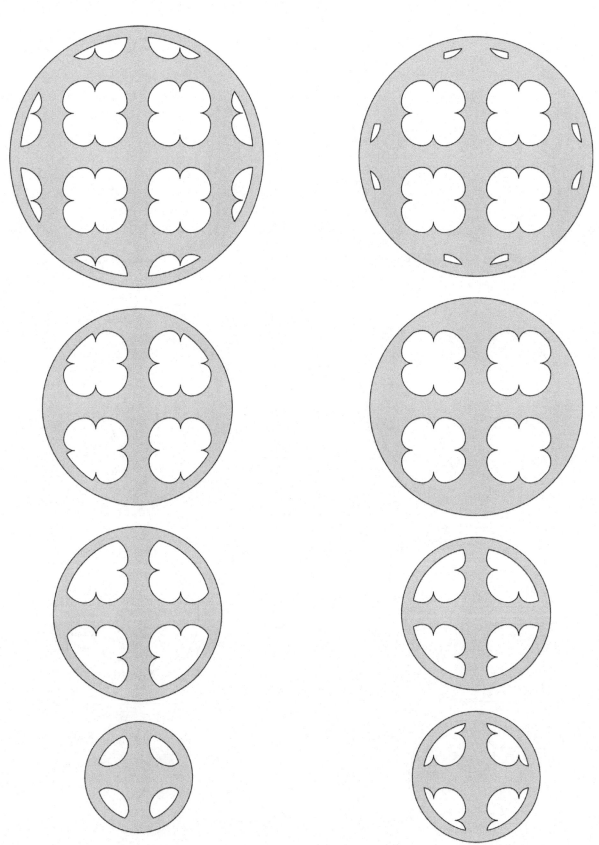

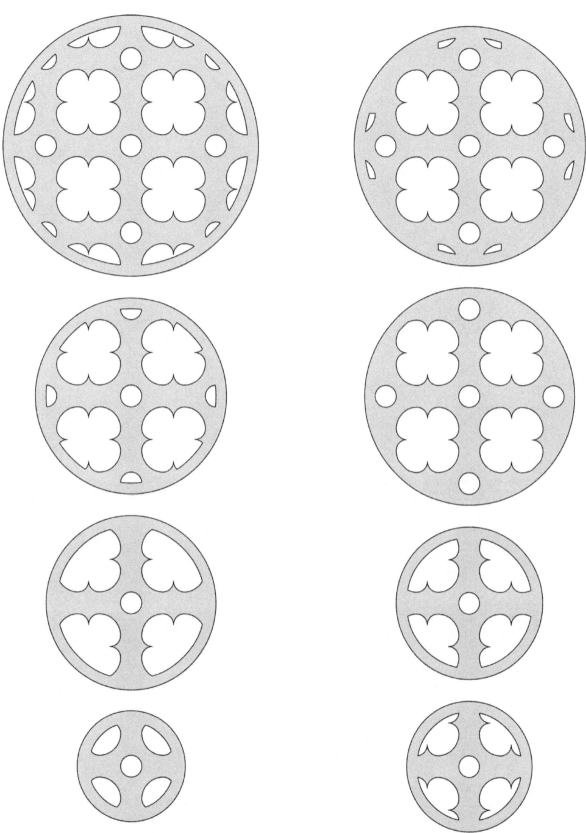

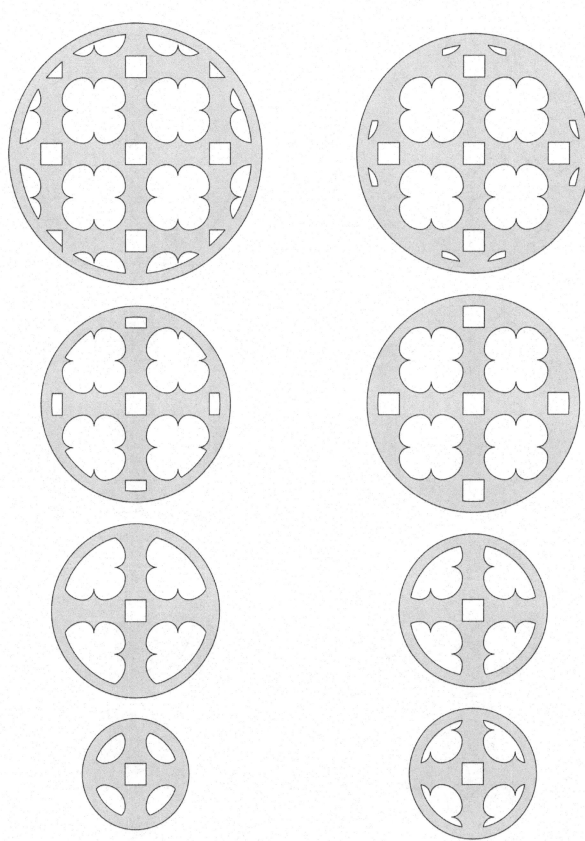

34

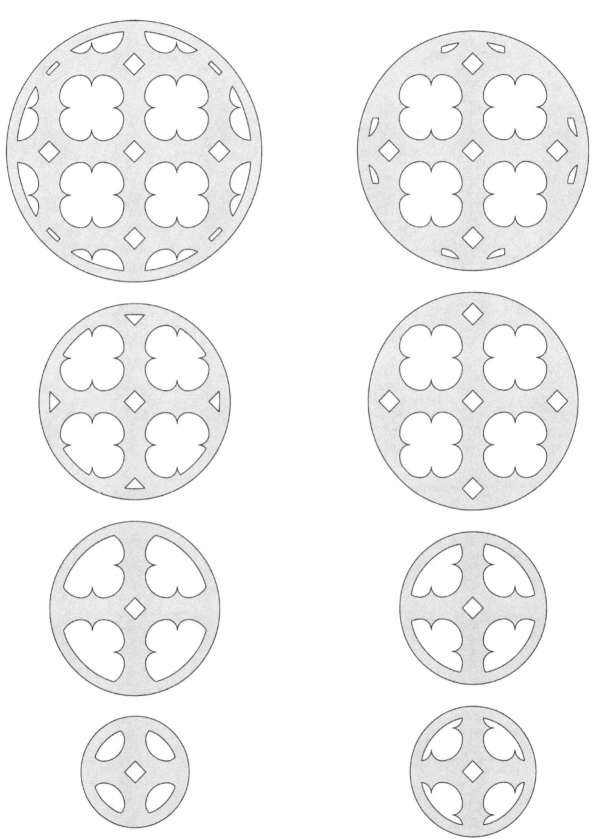

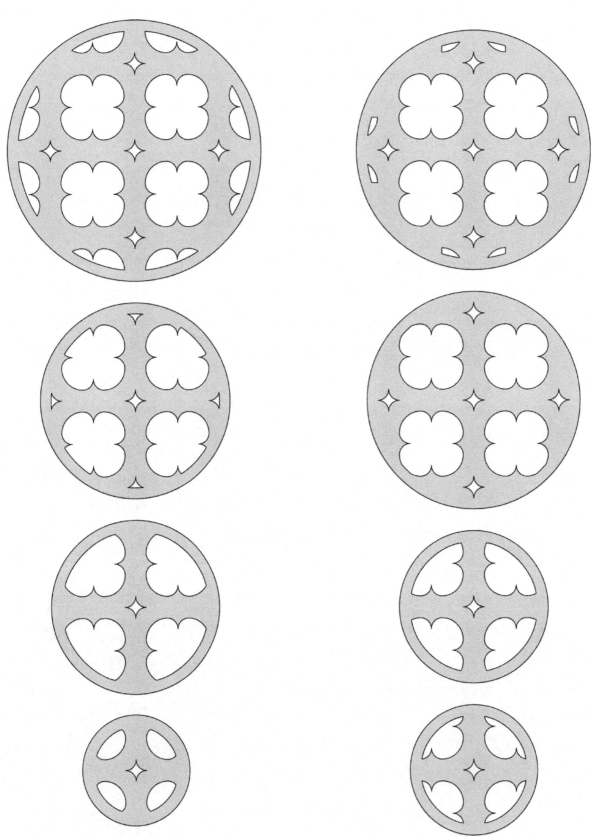

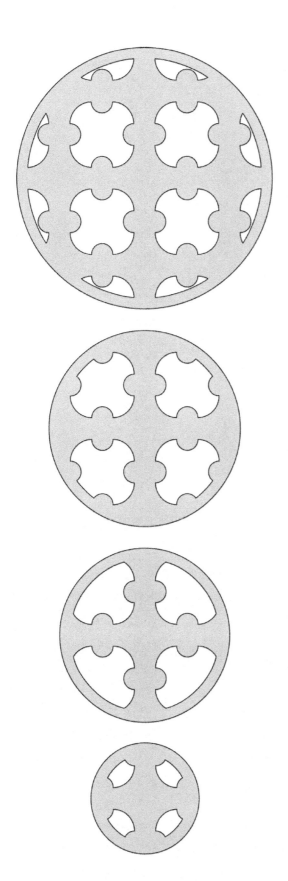
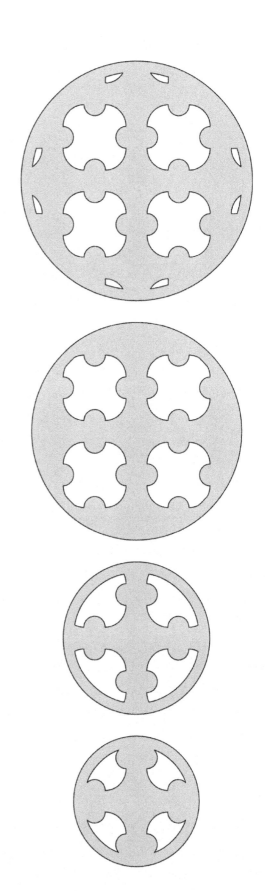

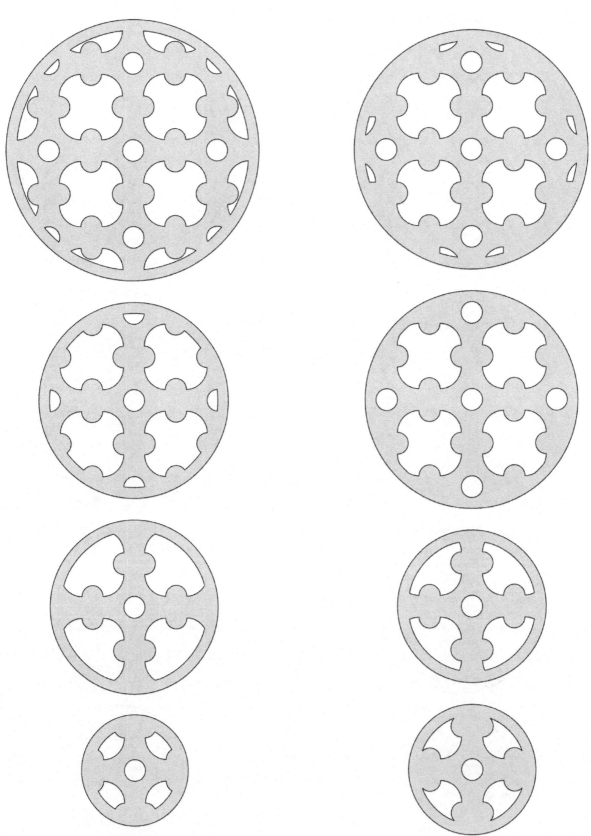

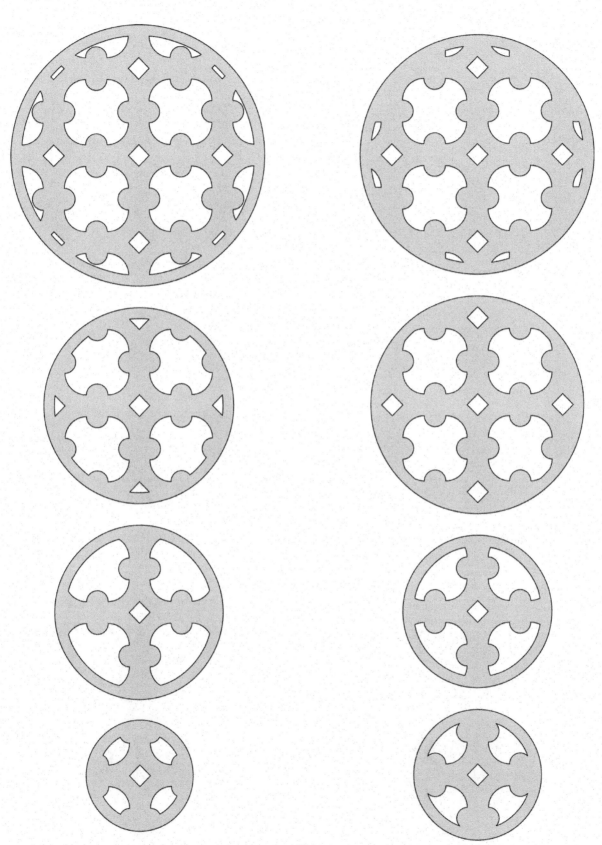

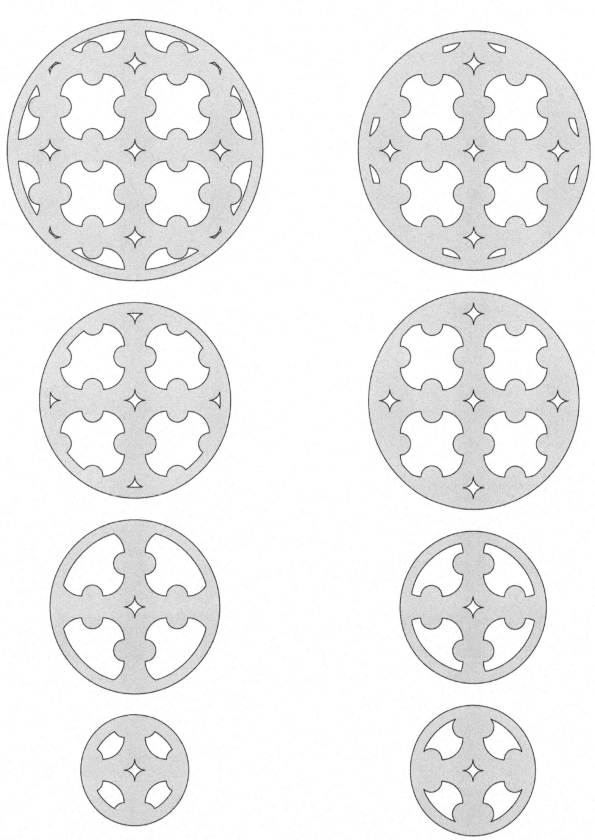

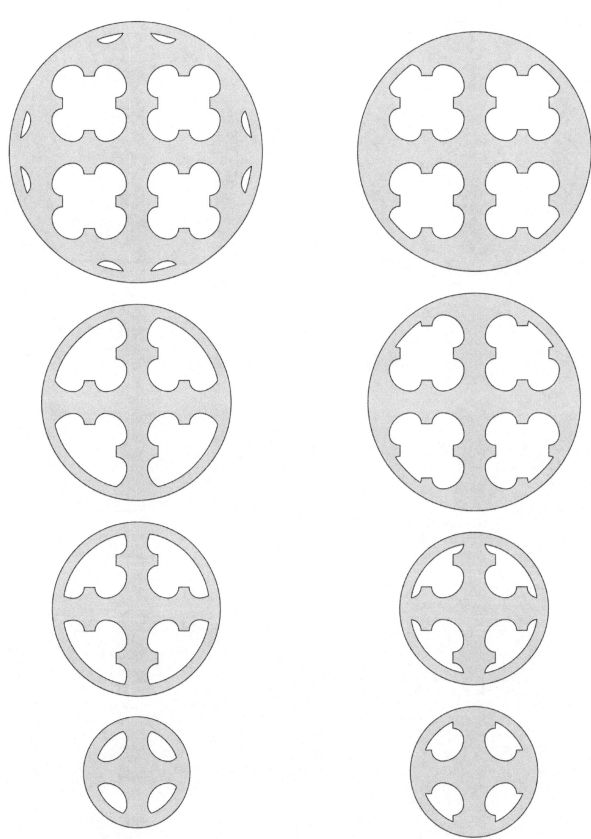

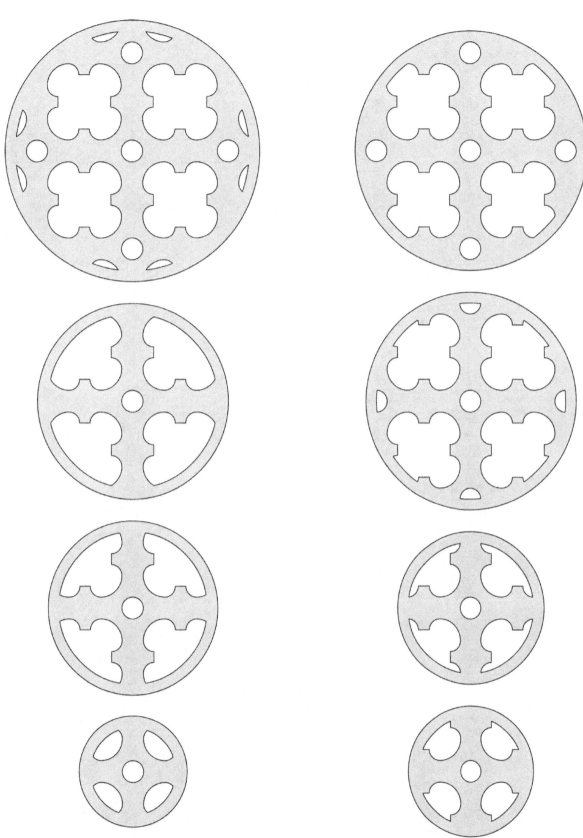

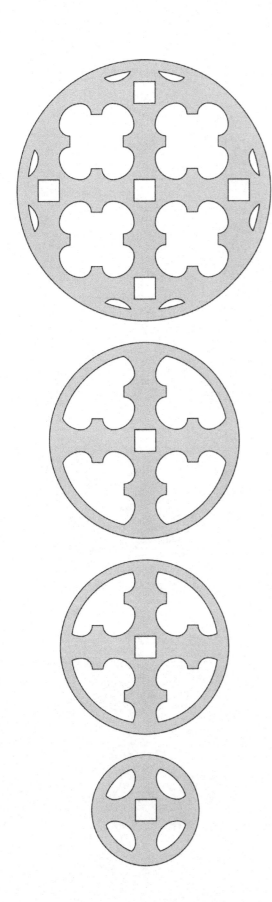
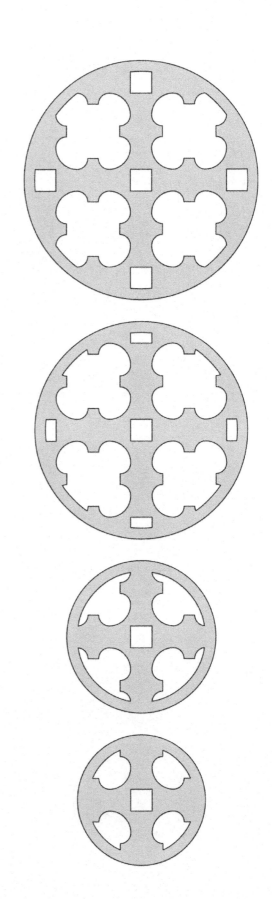

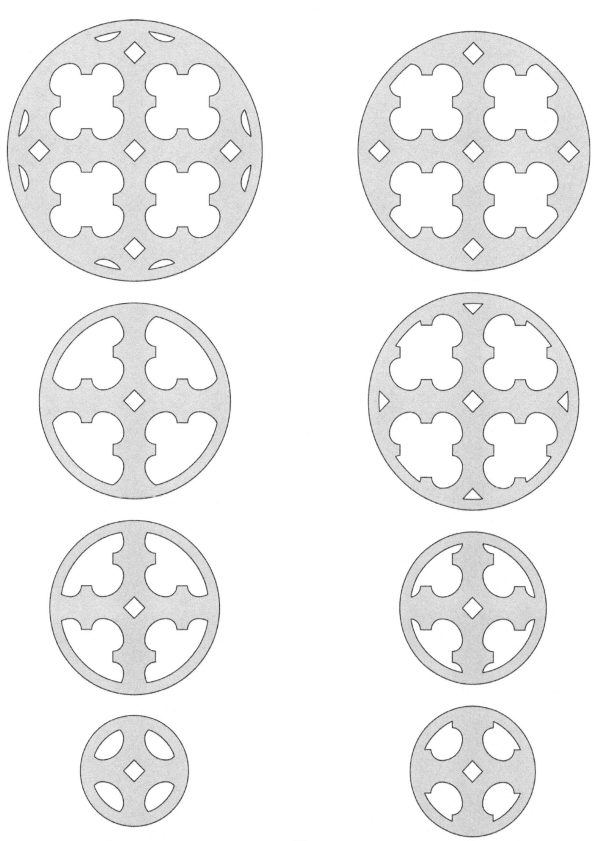

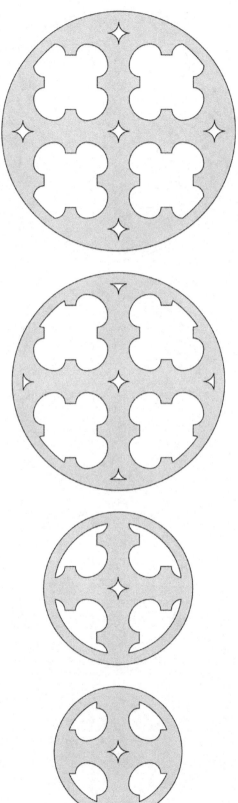

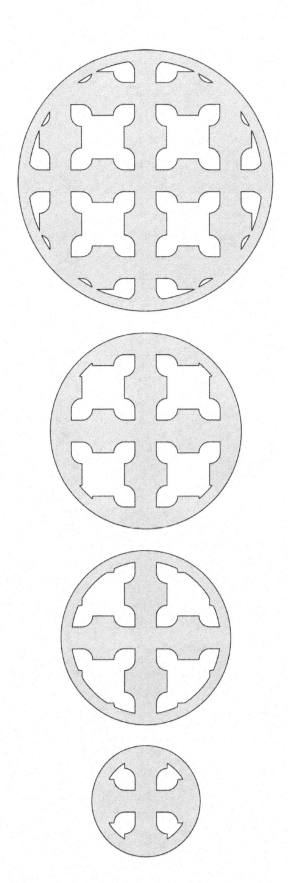
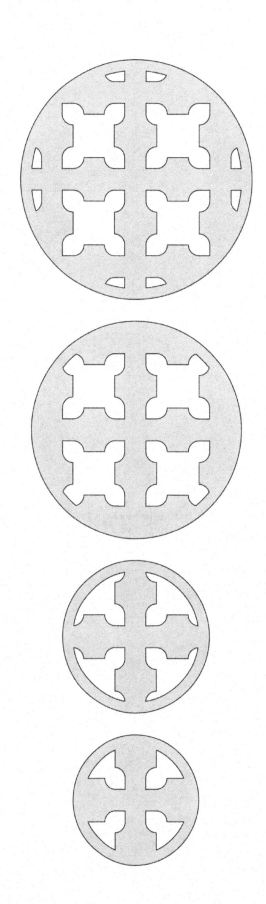

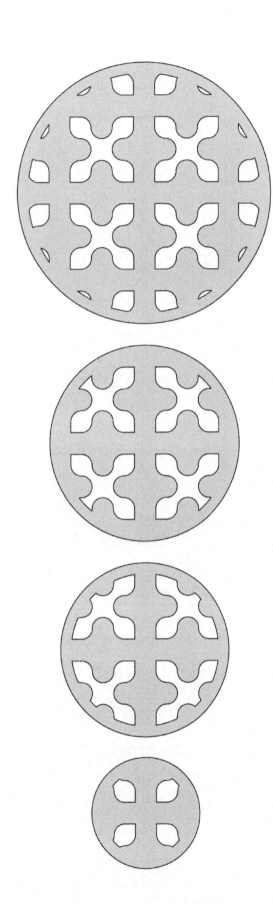
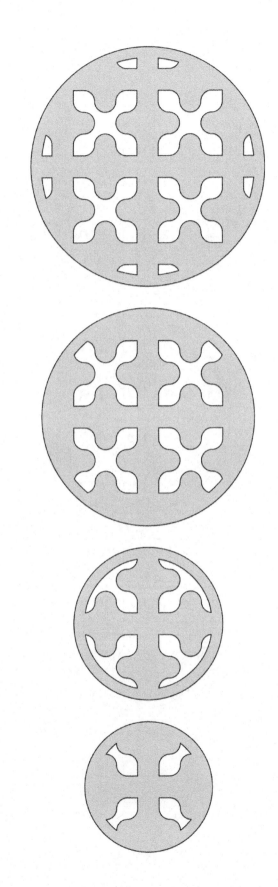

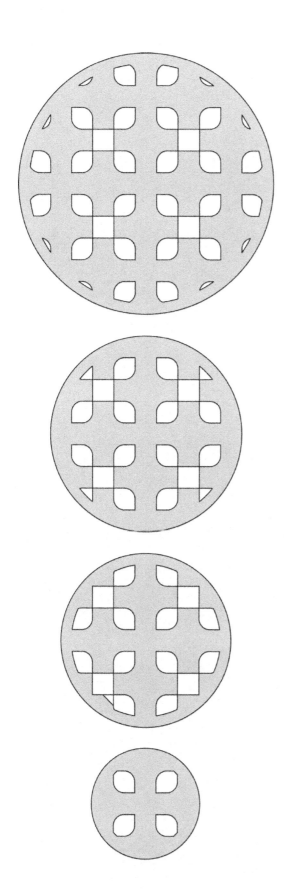
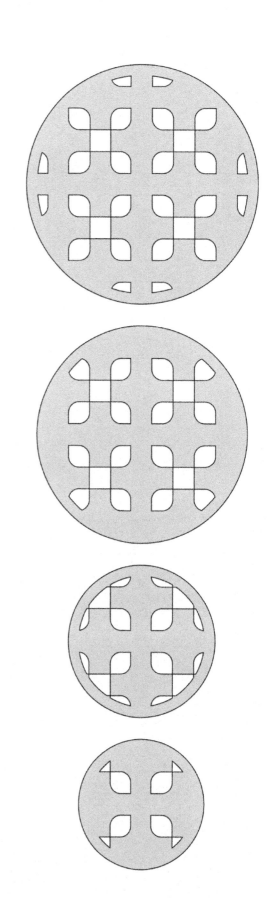

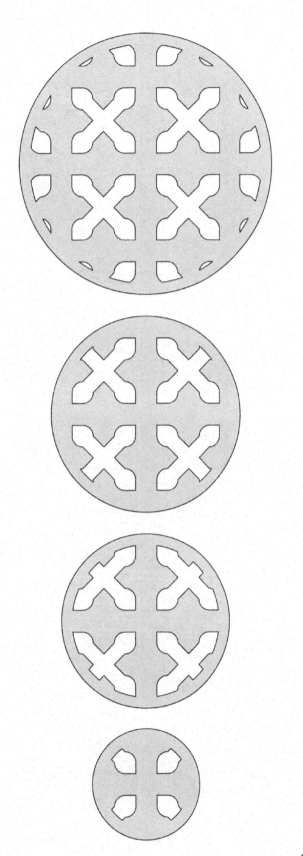
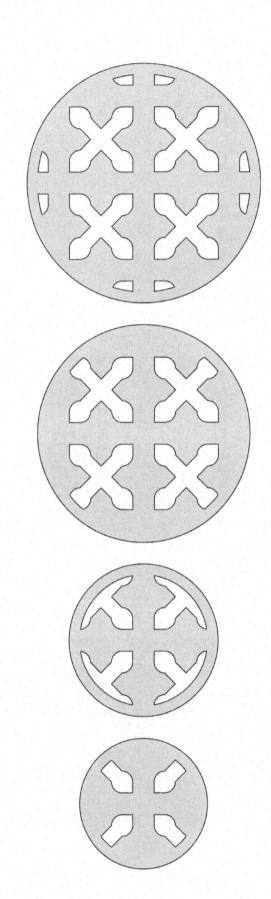

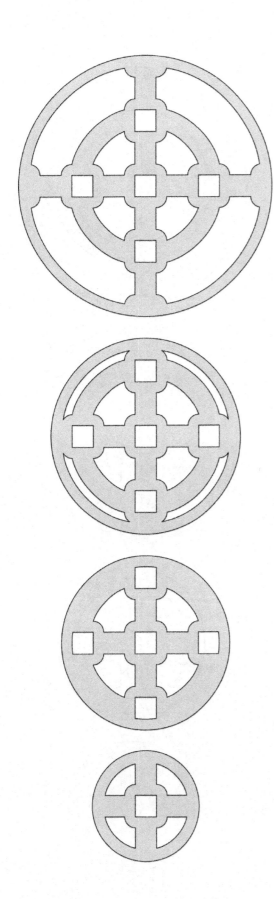

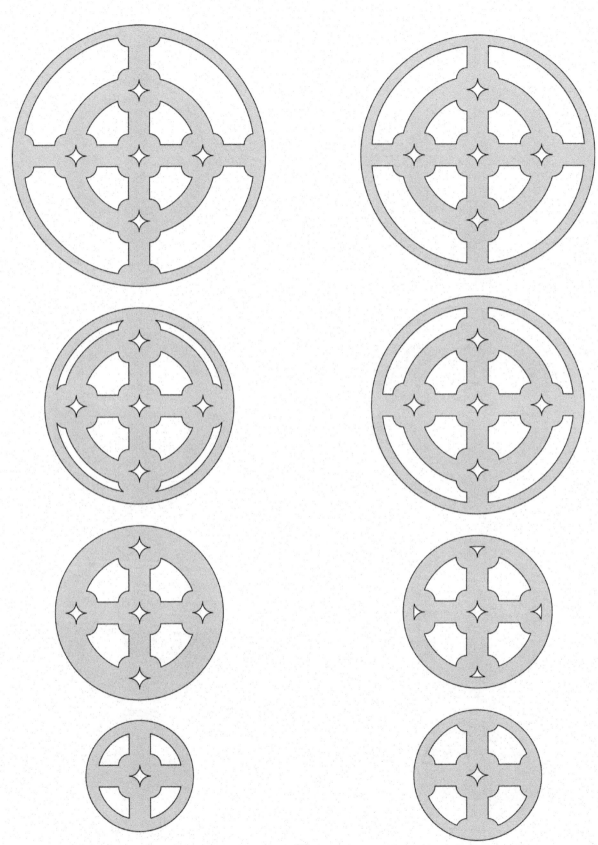

56

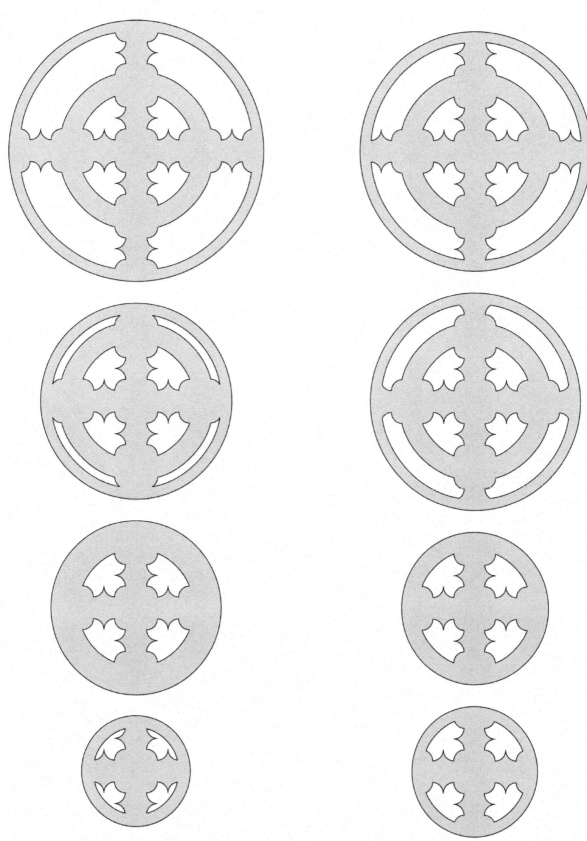

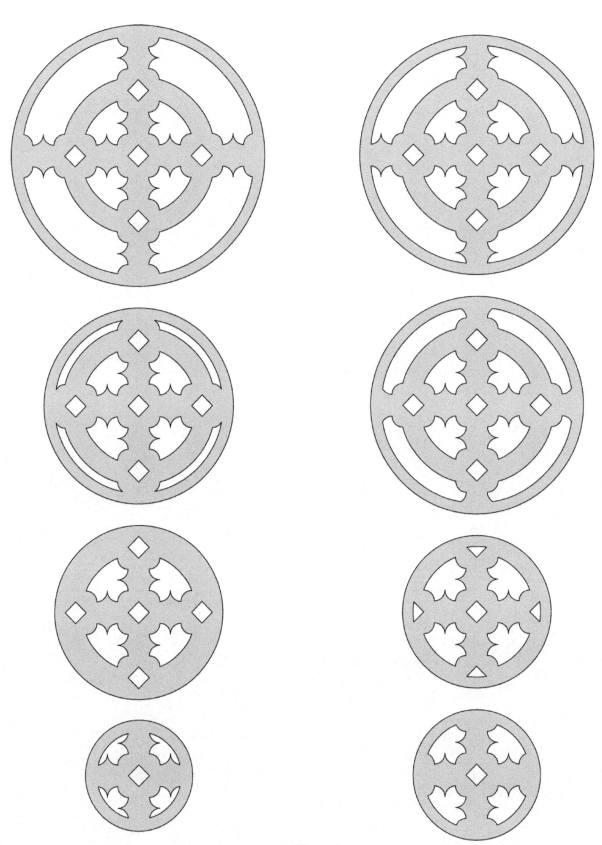

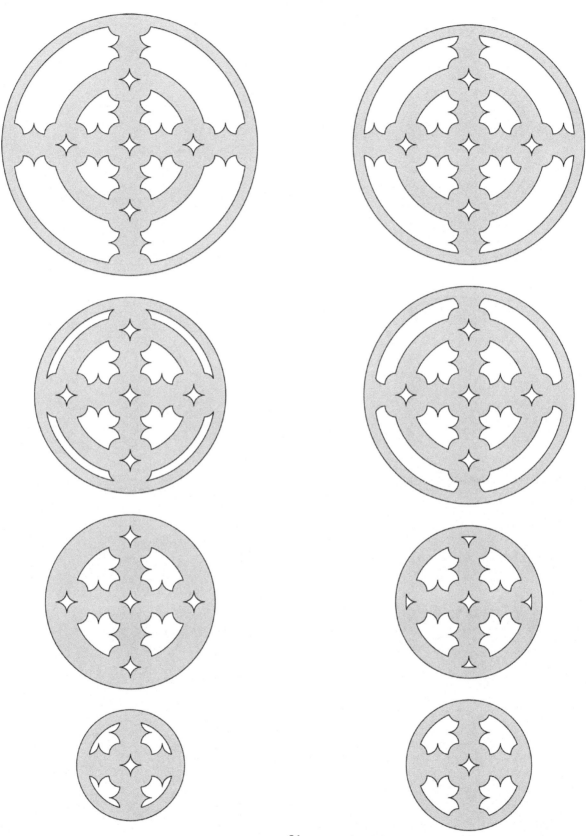

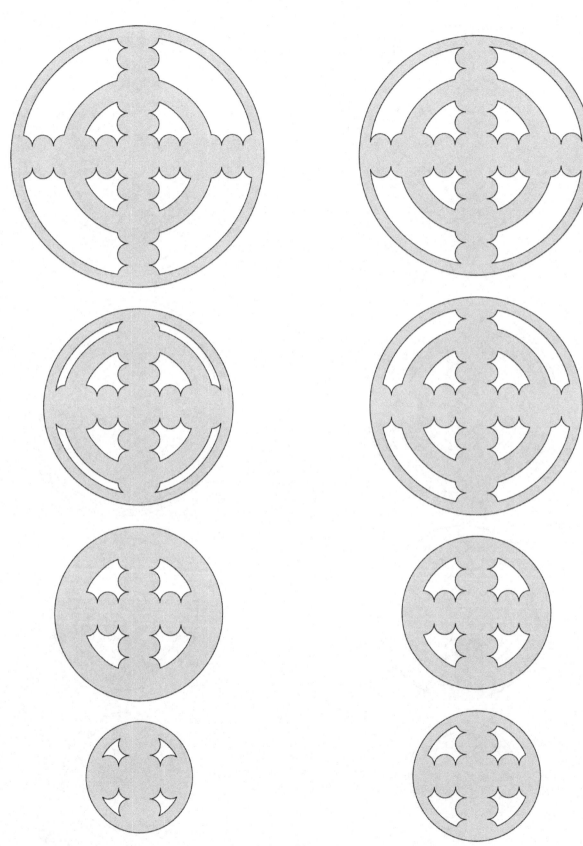

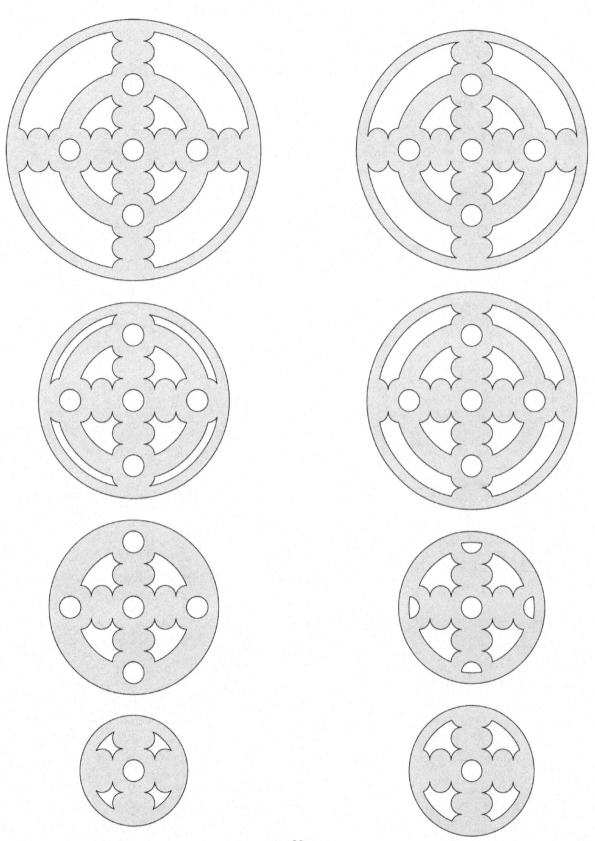

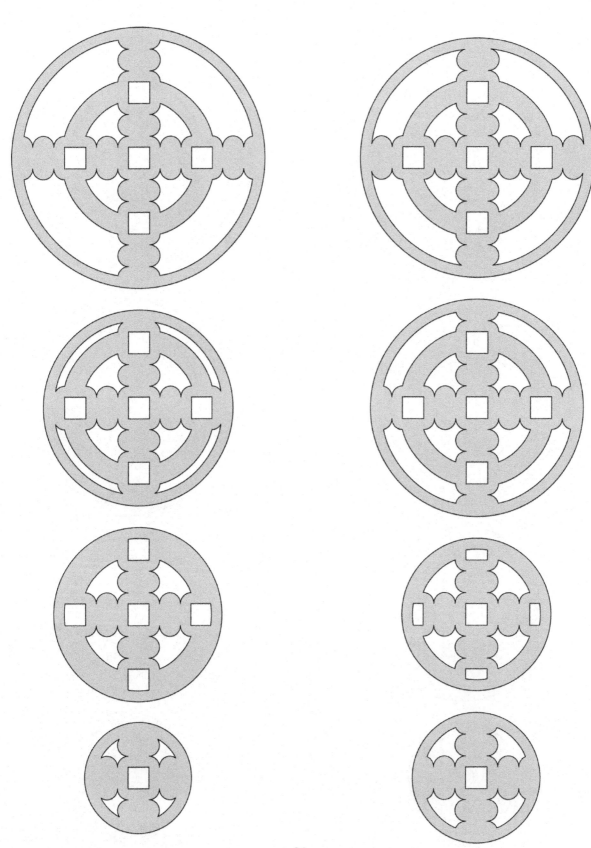

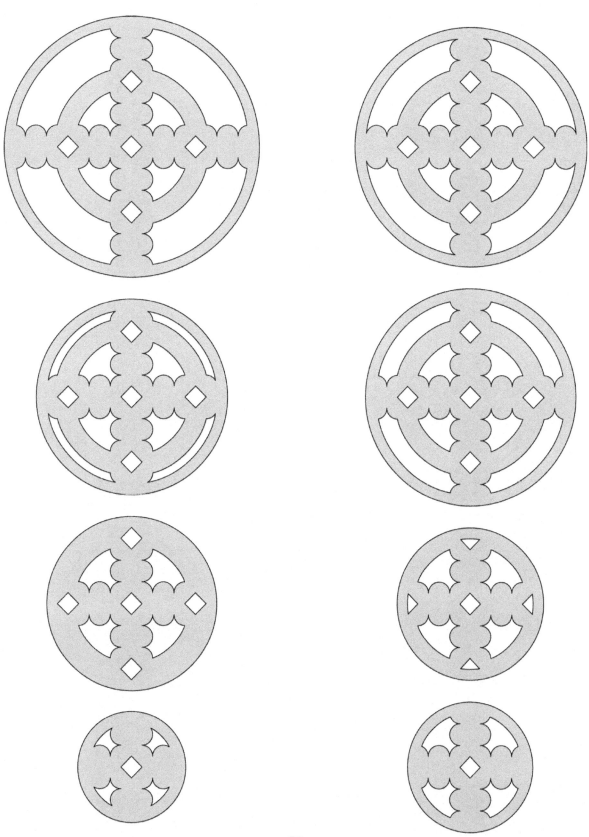

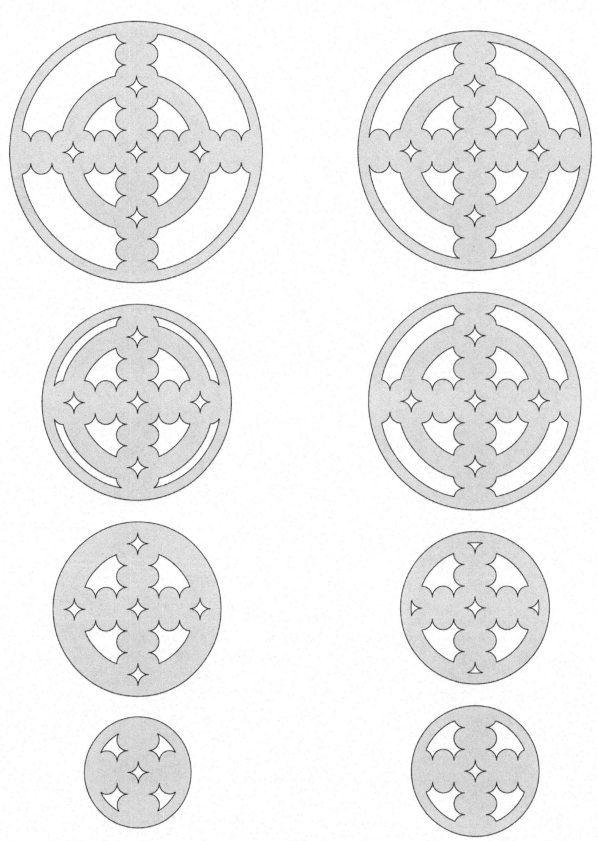

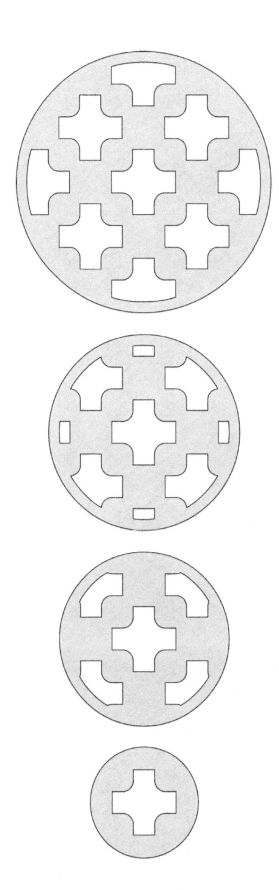

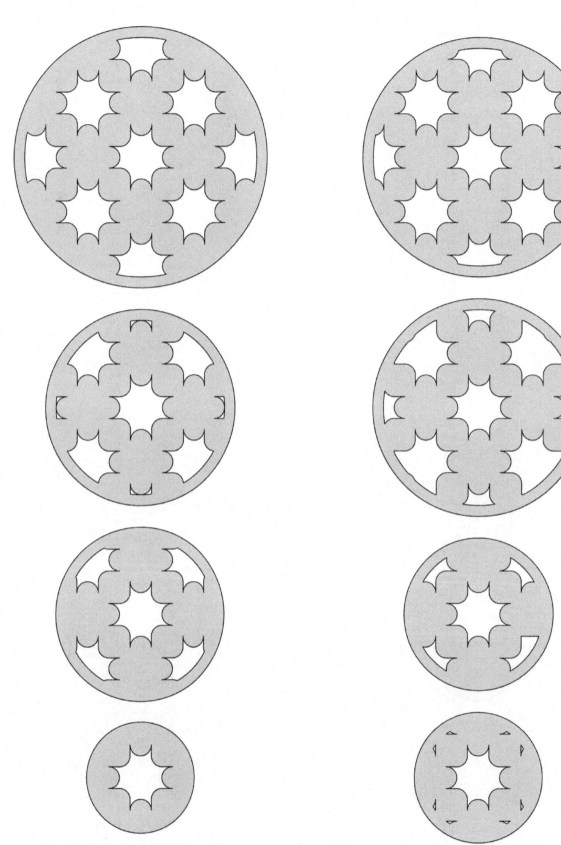

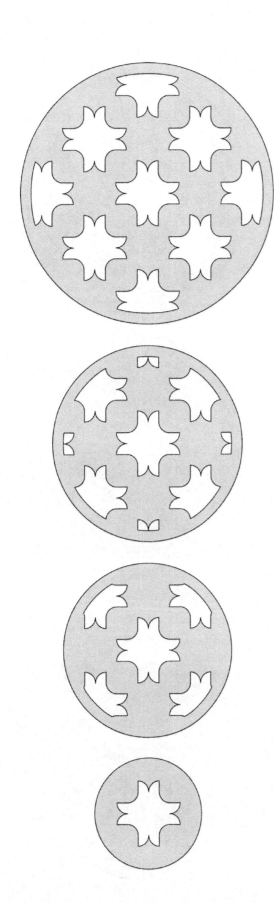
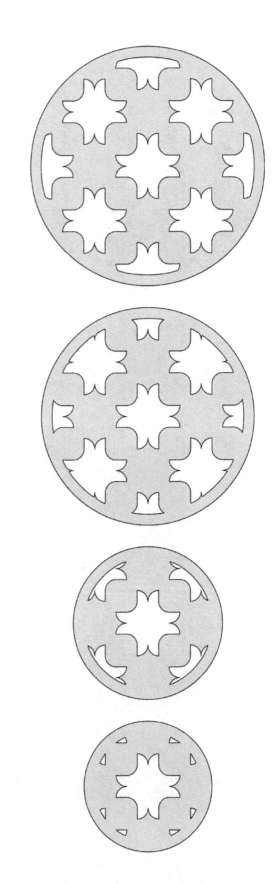

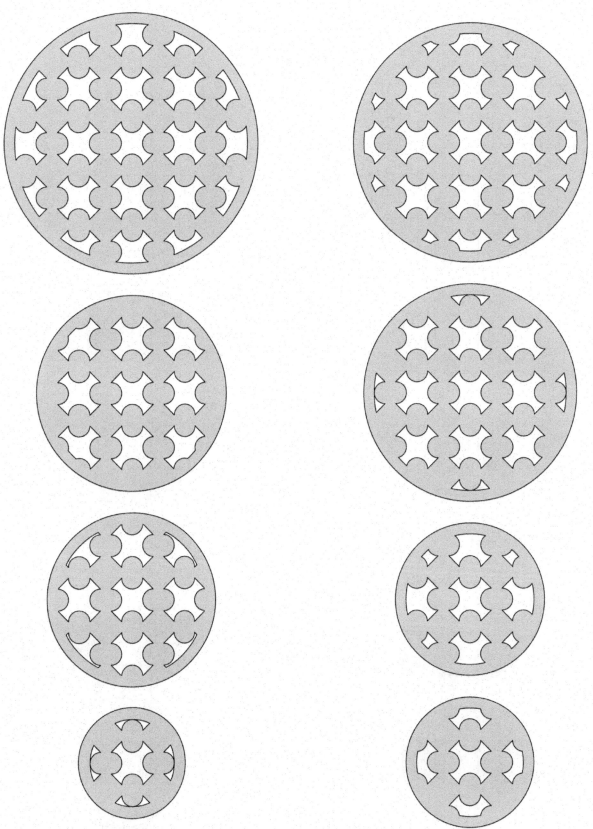

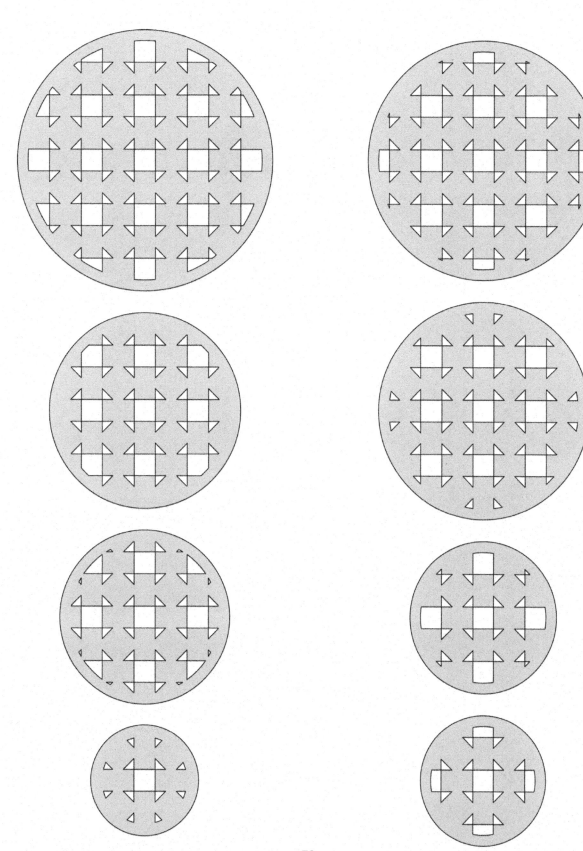

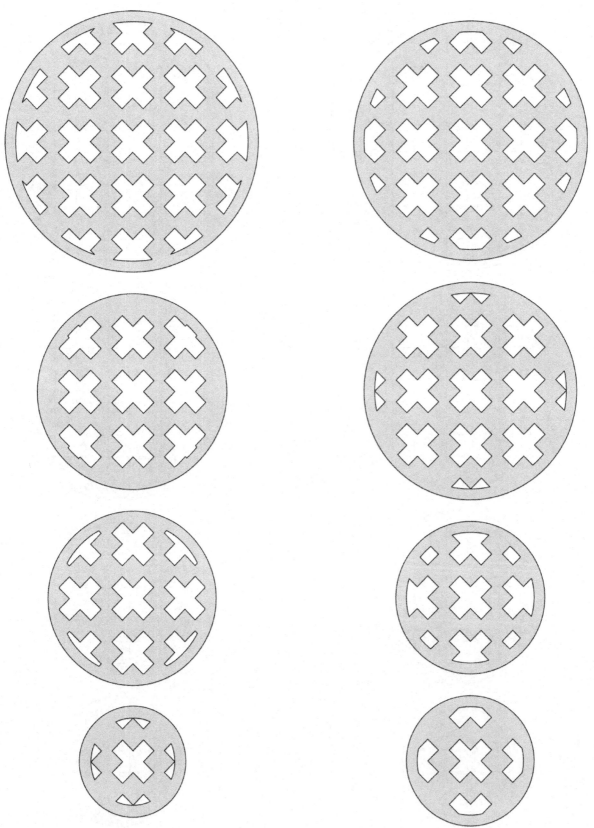

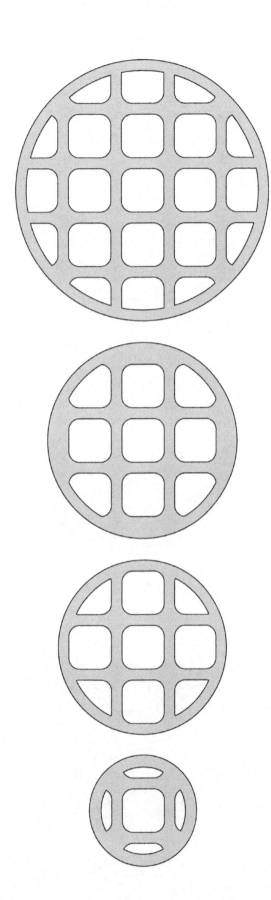

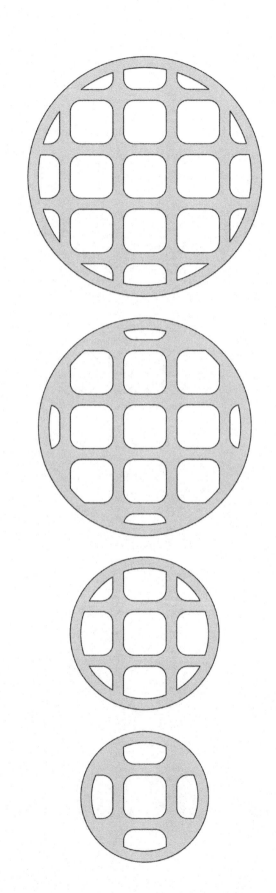

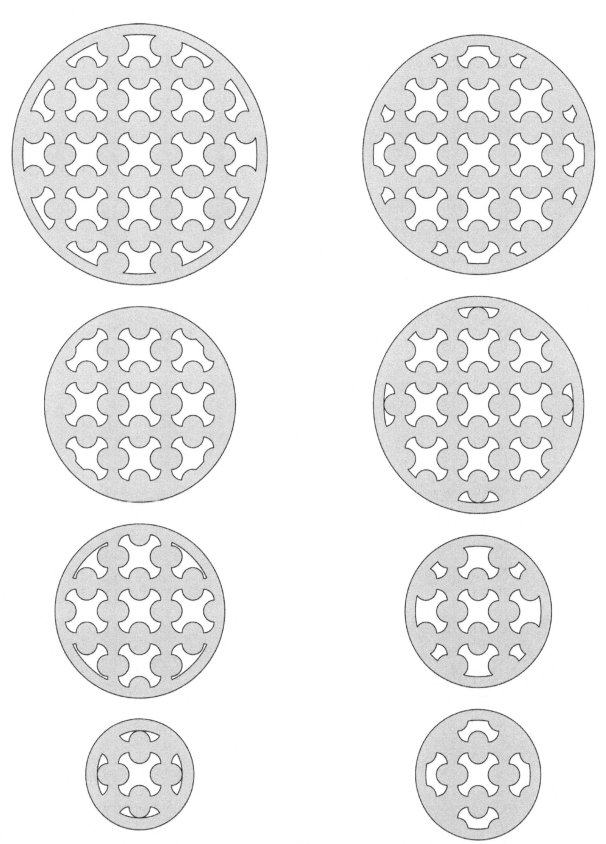

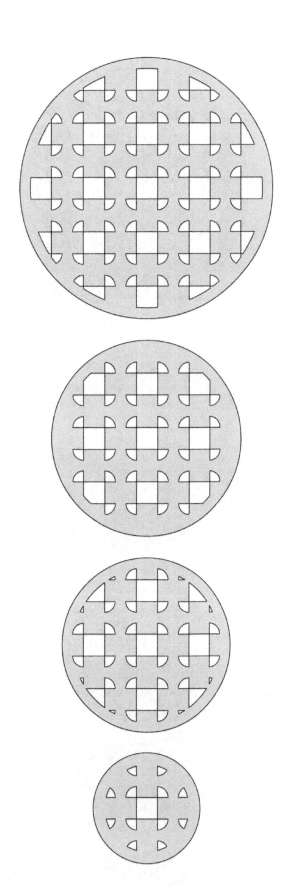

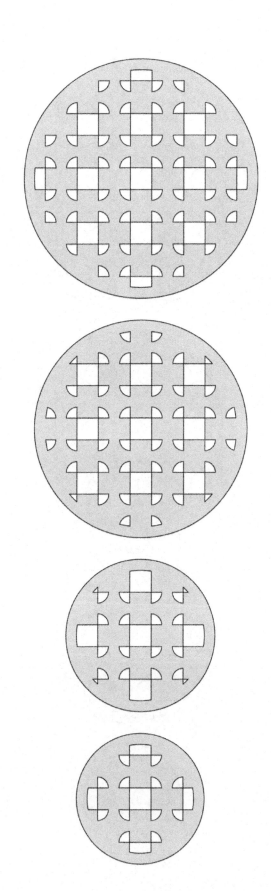

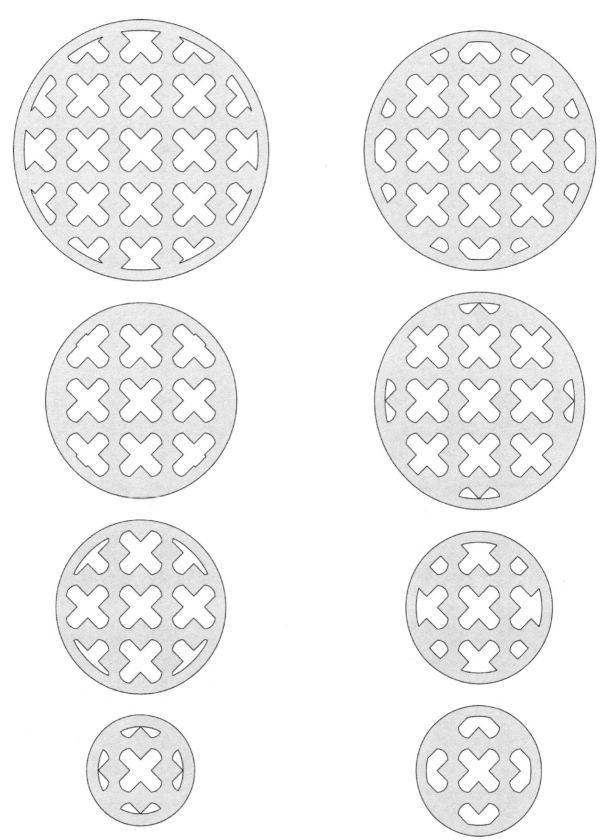

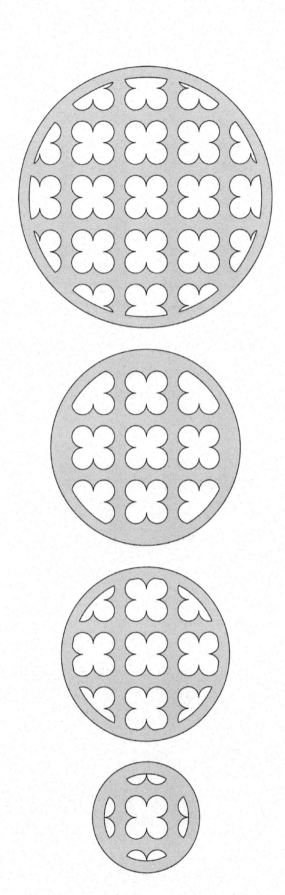
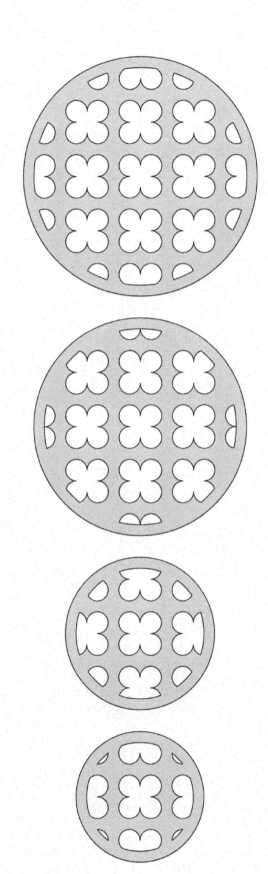

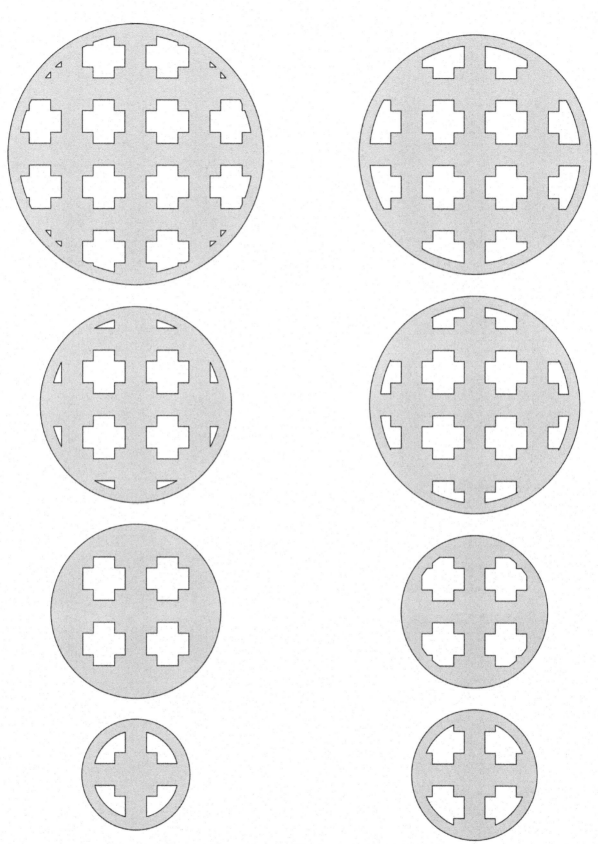

81

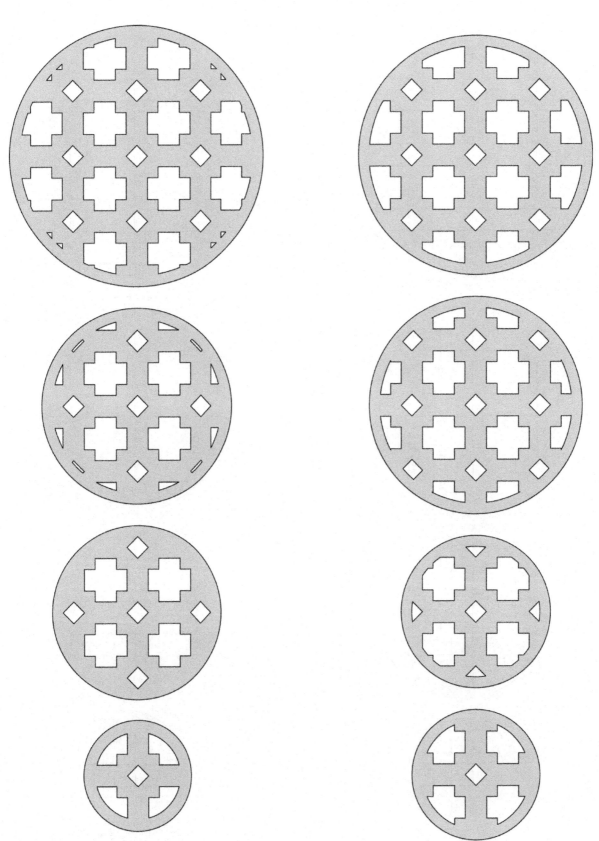

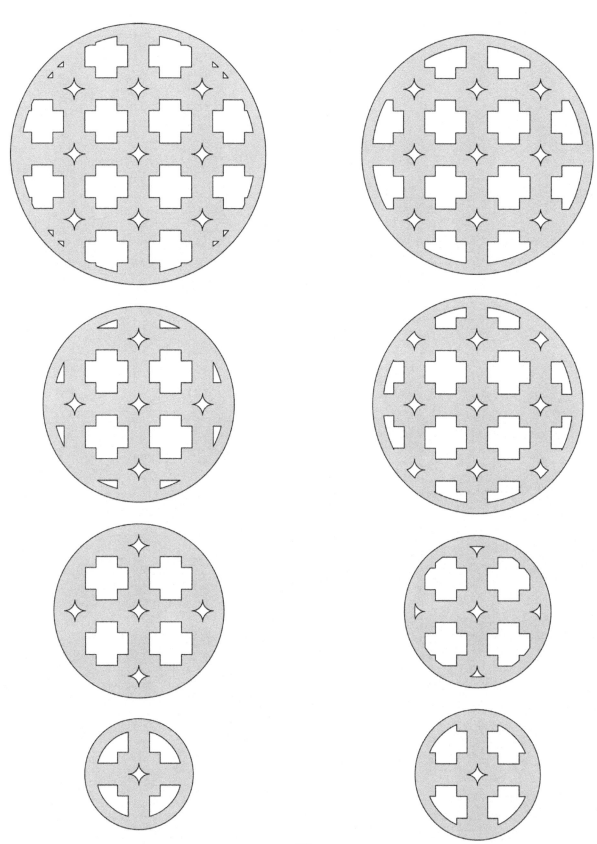

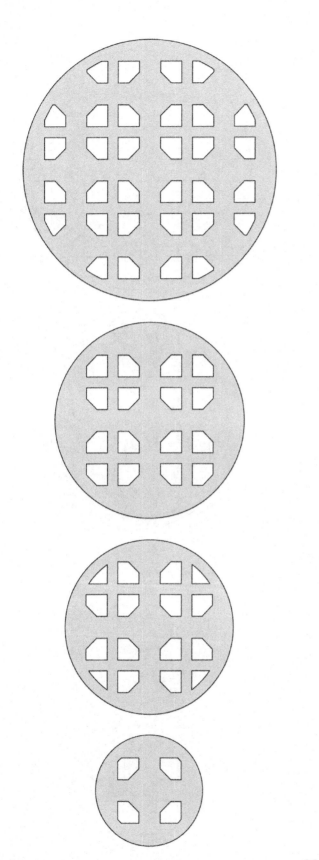
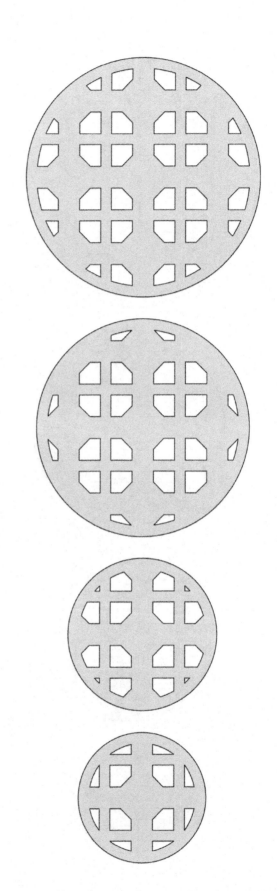

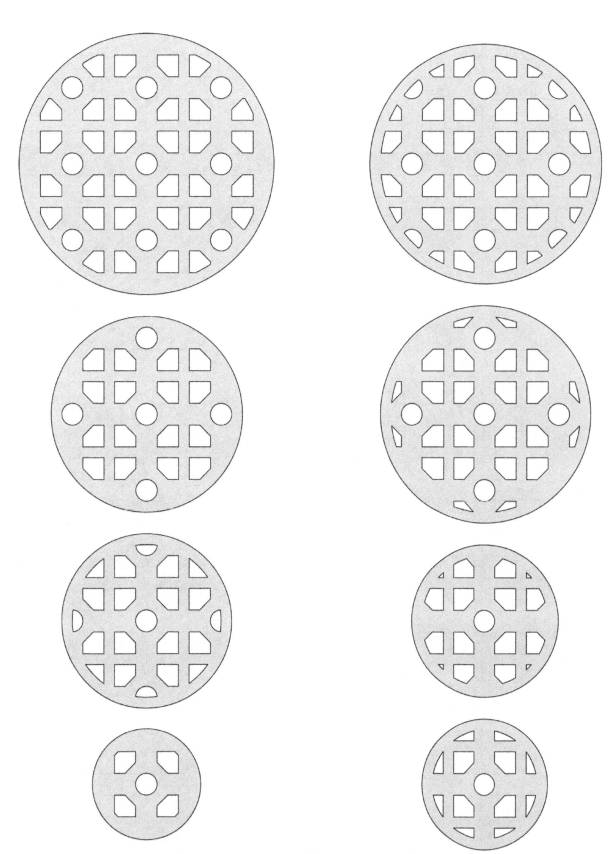

88

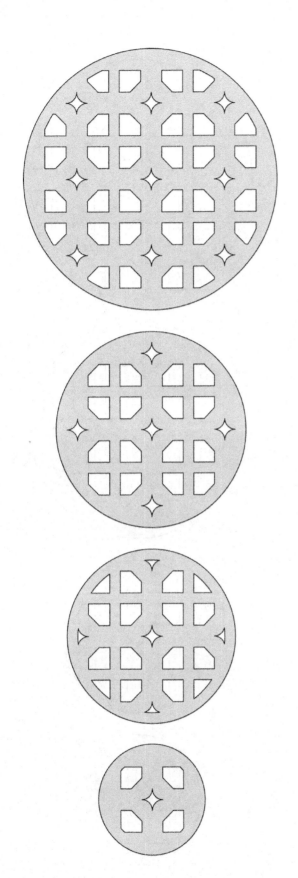
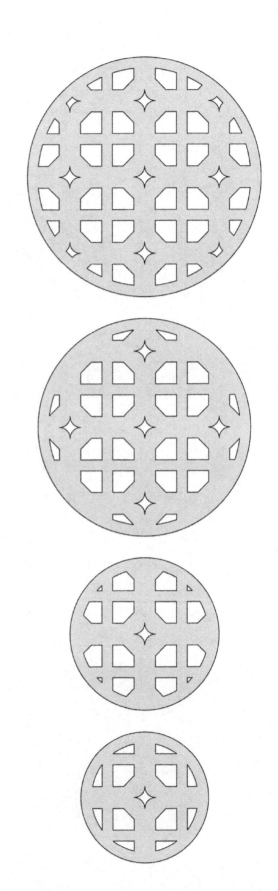

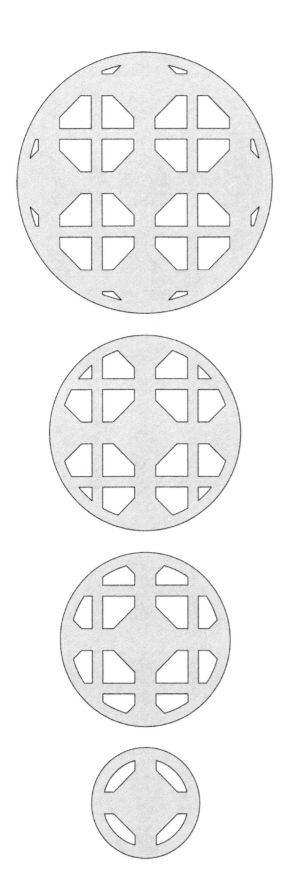
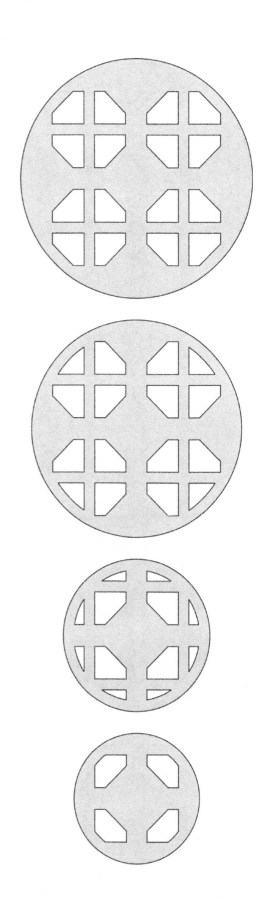

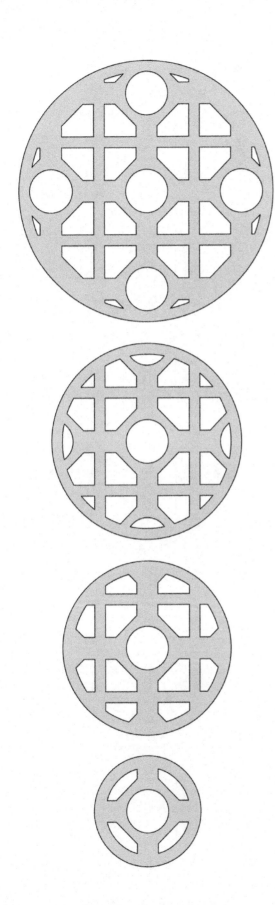
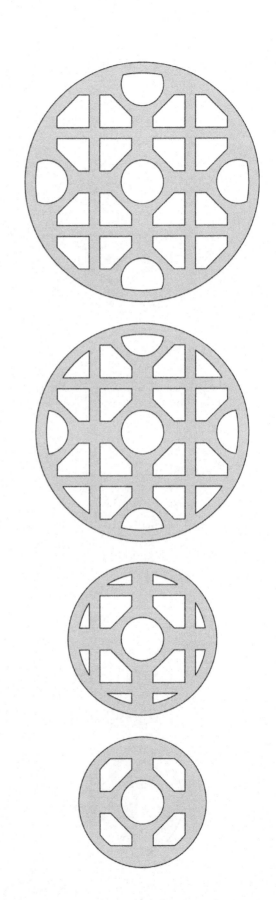

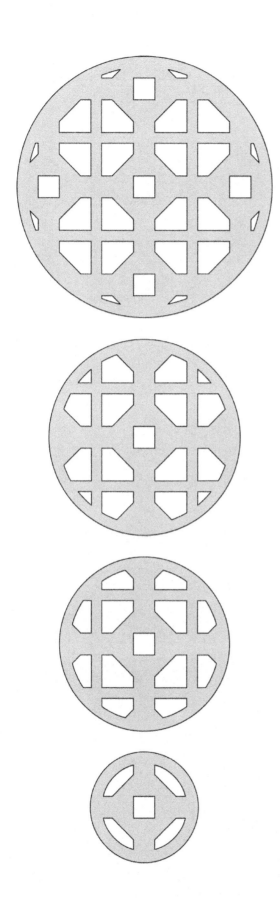
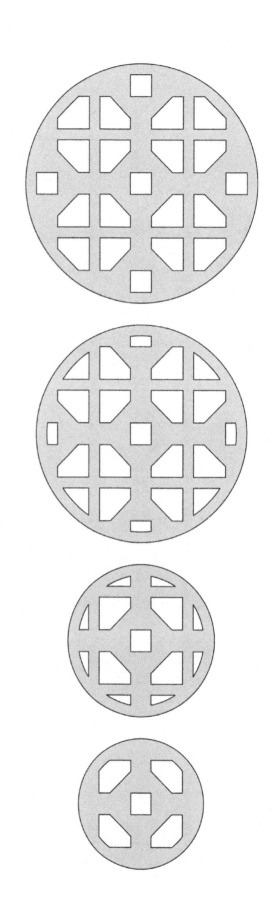

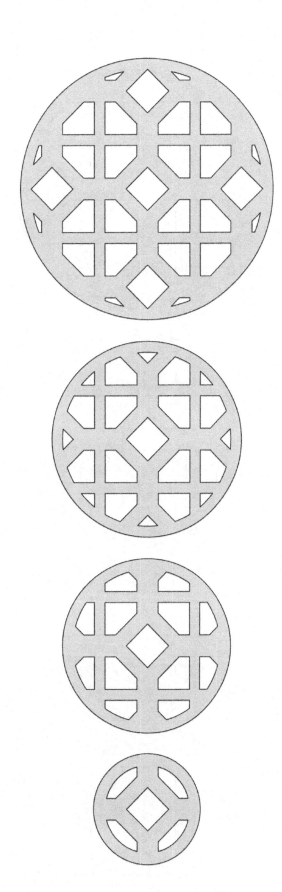
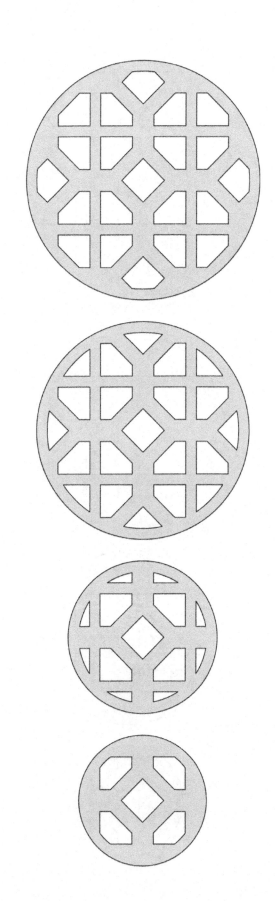

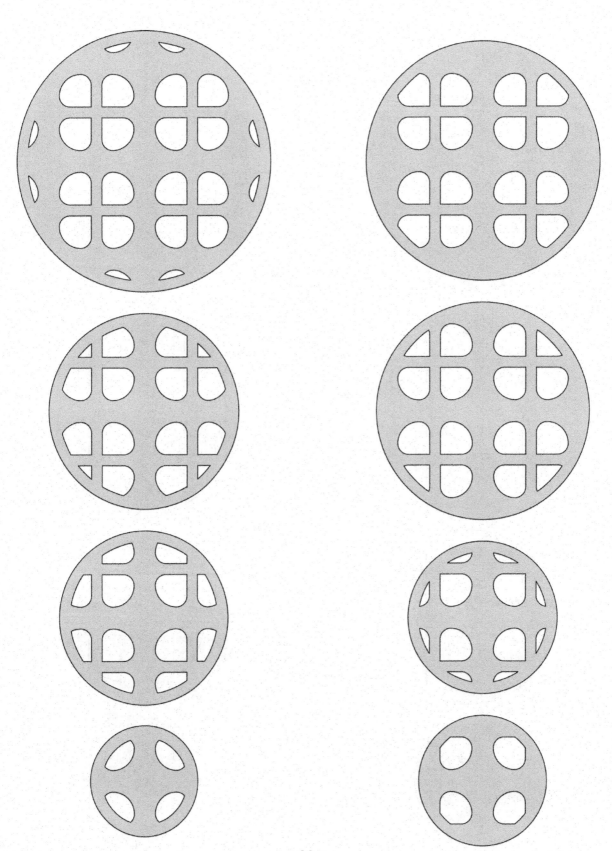

97

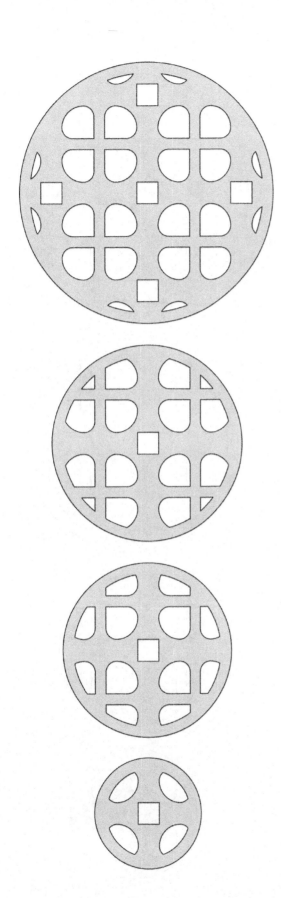
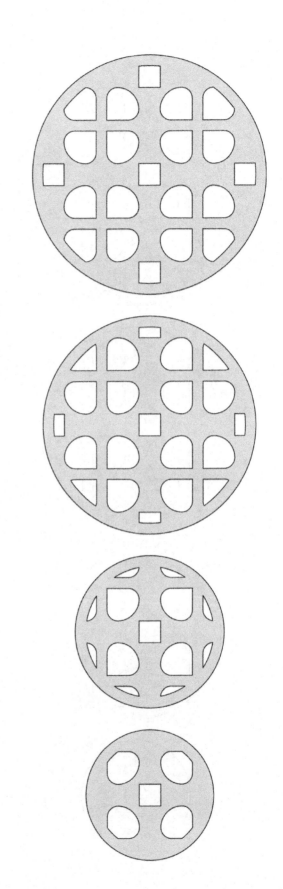

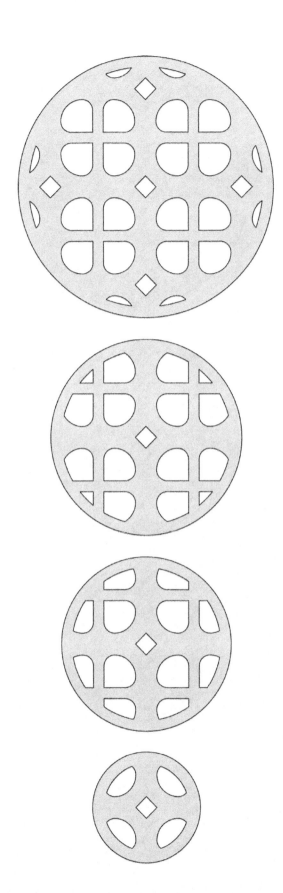
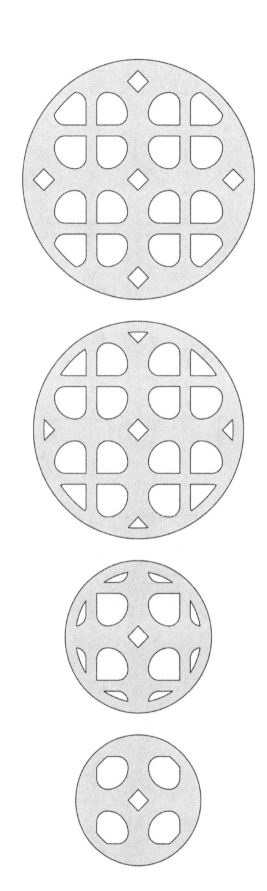

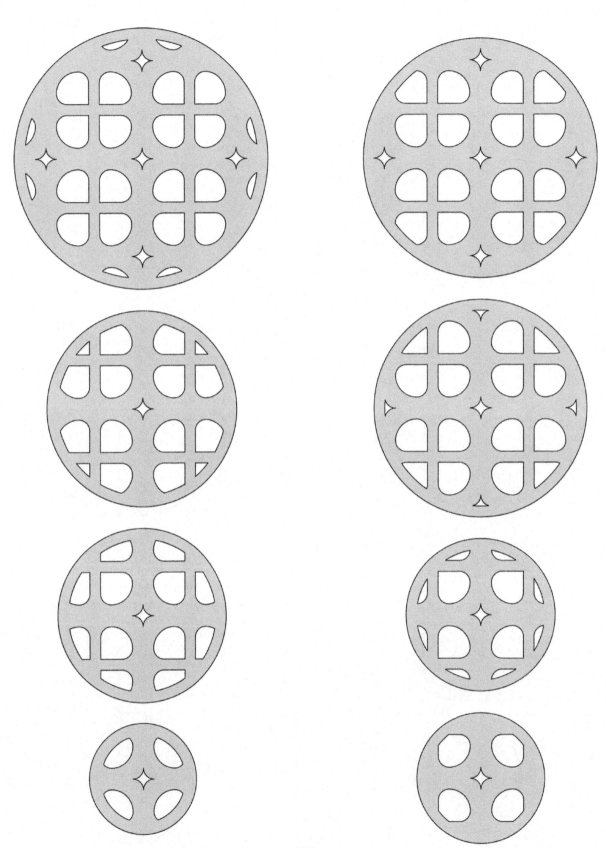

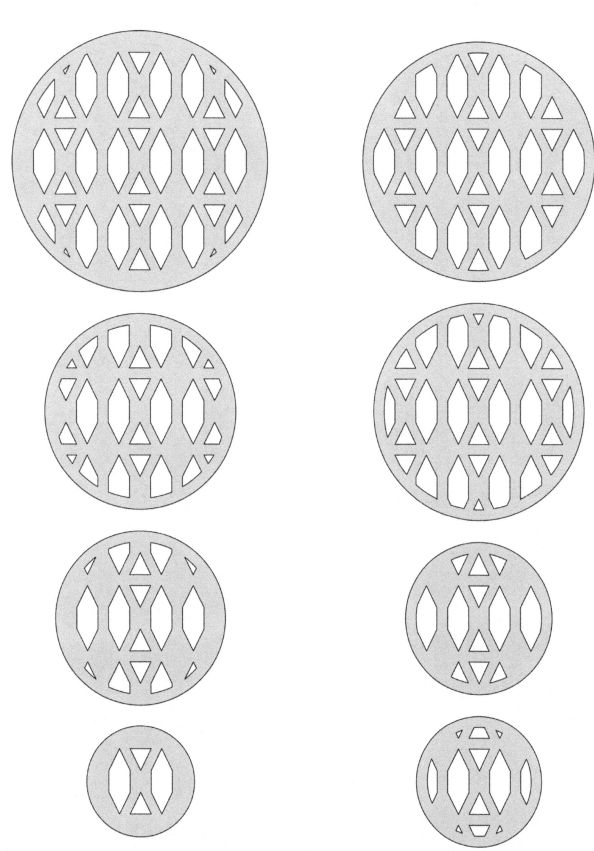

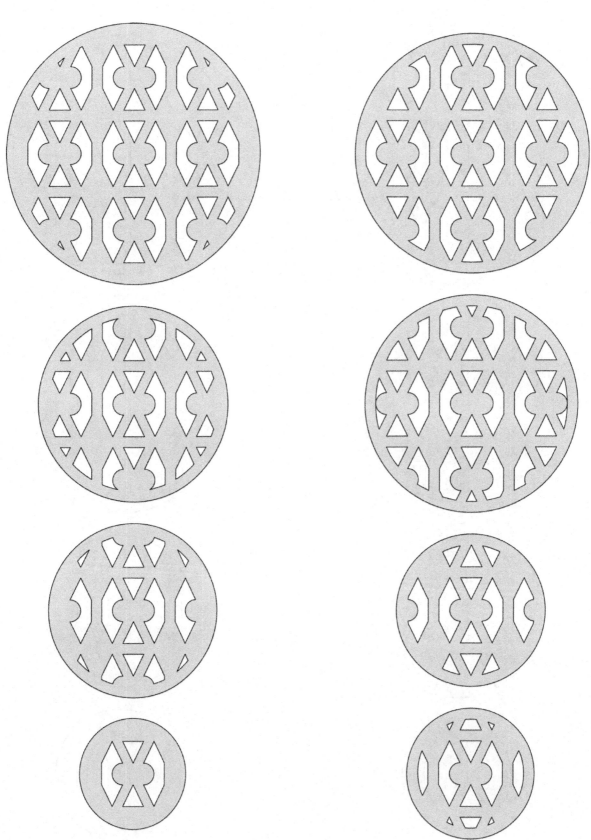

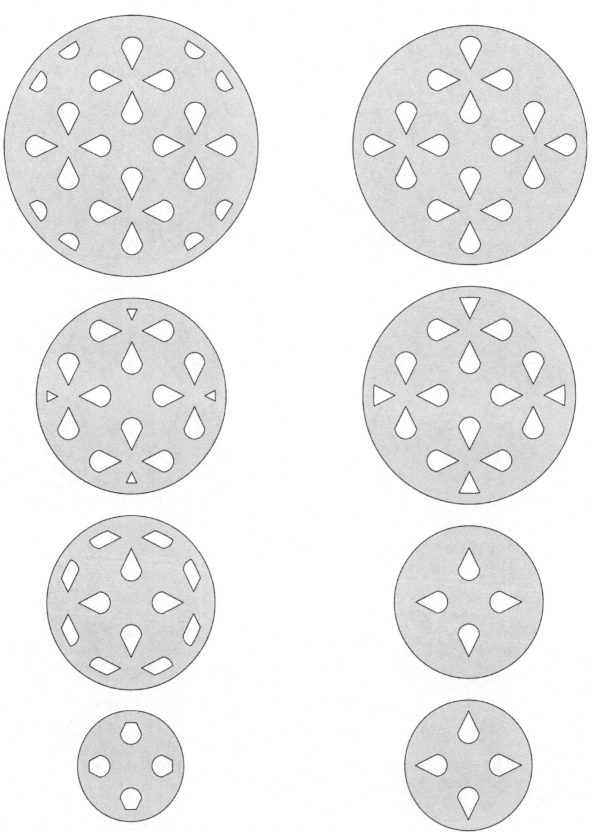

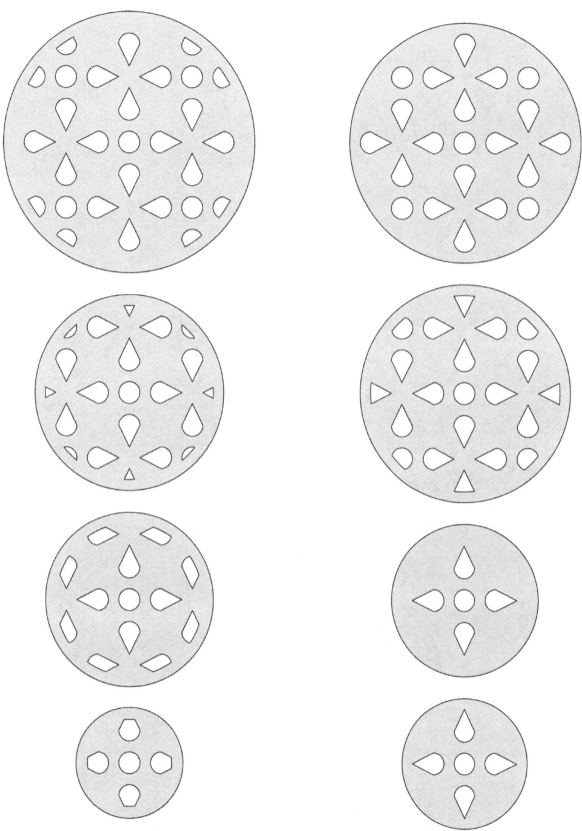

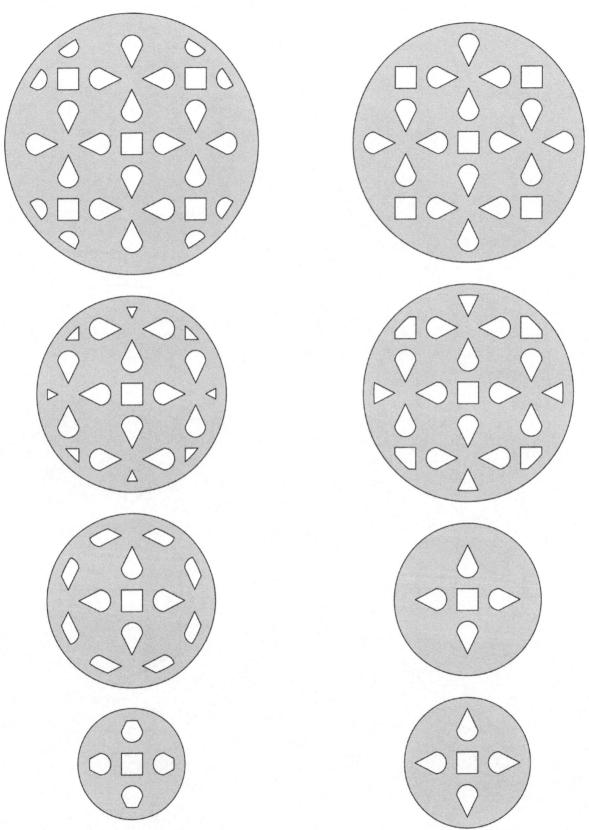

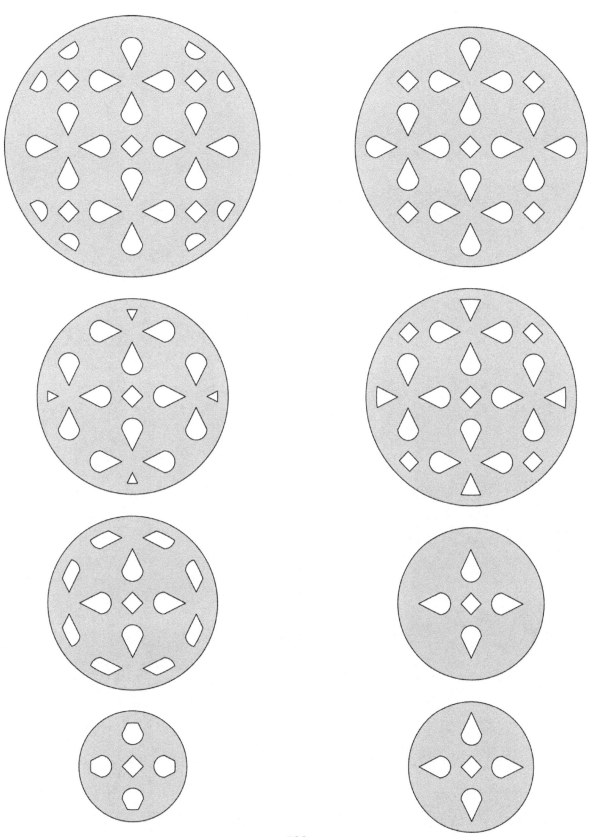

109

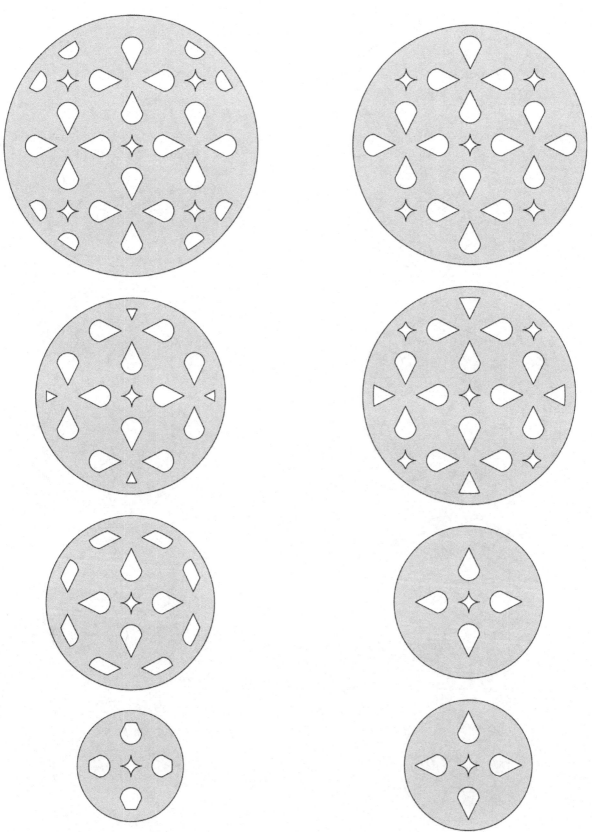

111

113

114

115

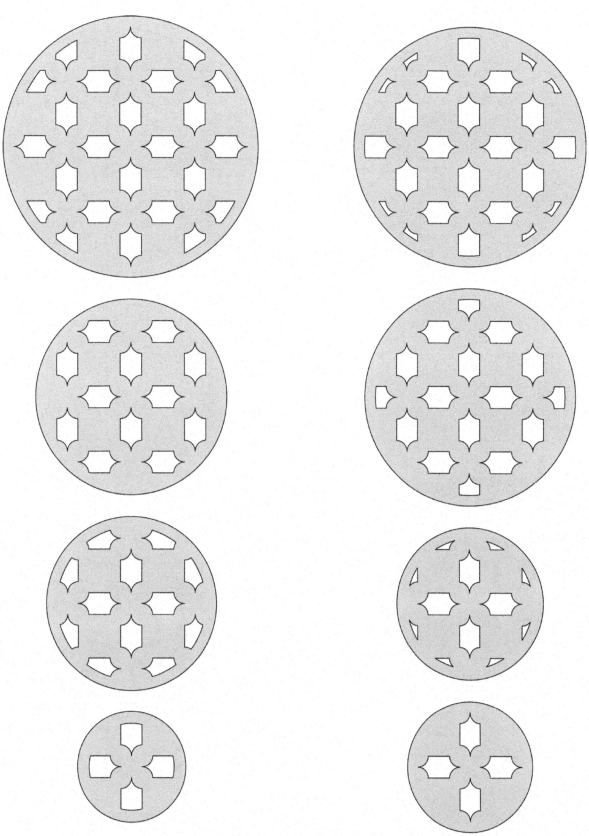

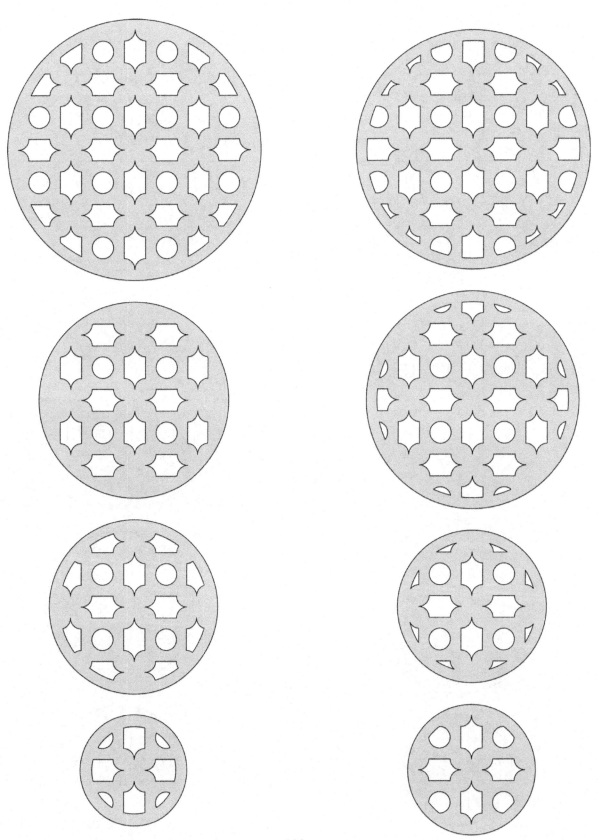

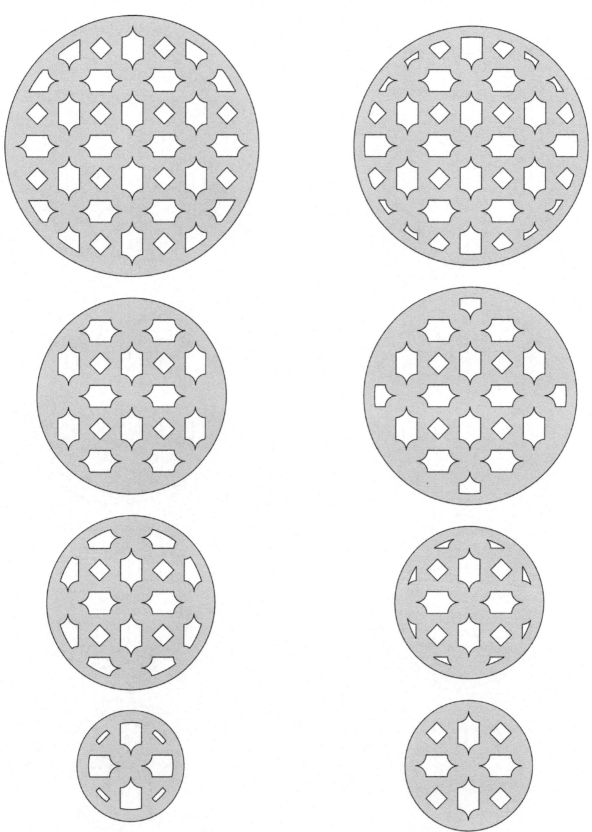

124

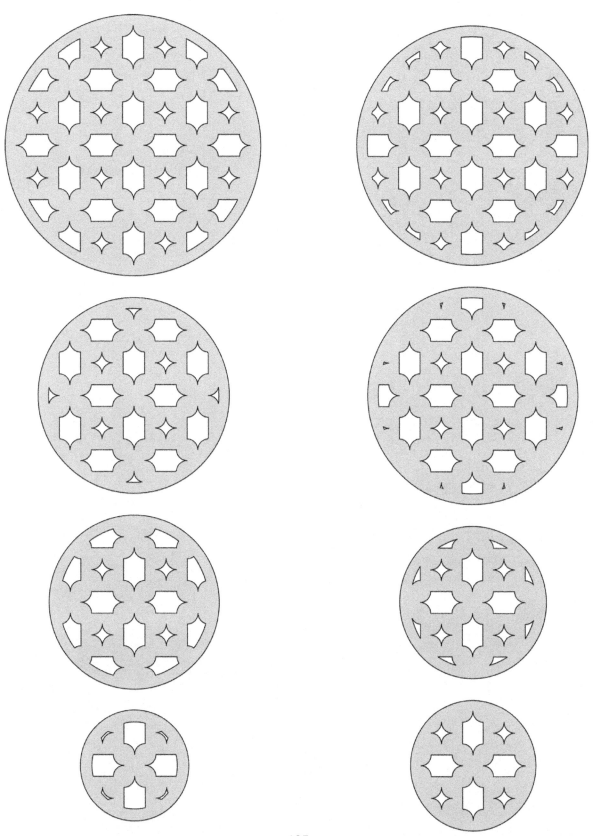

125

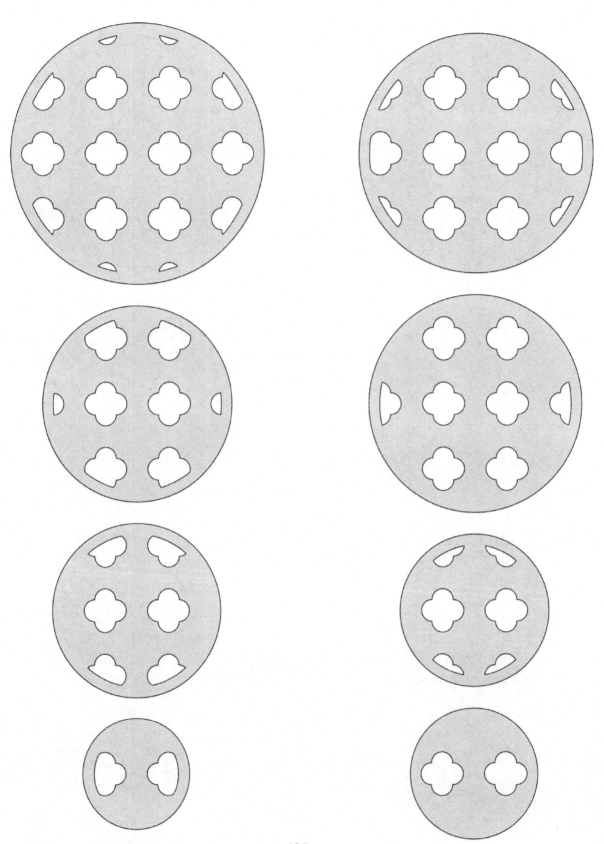

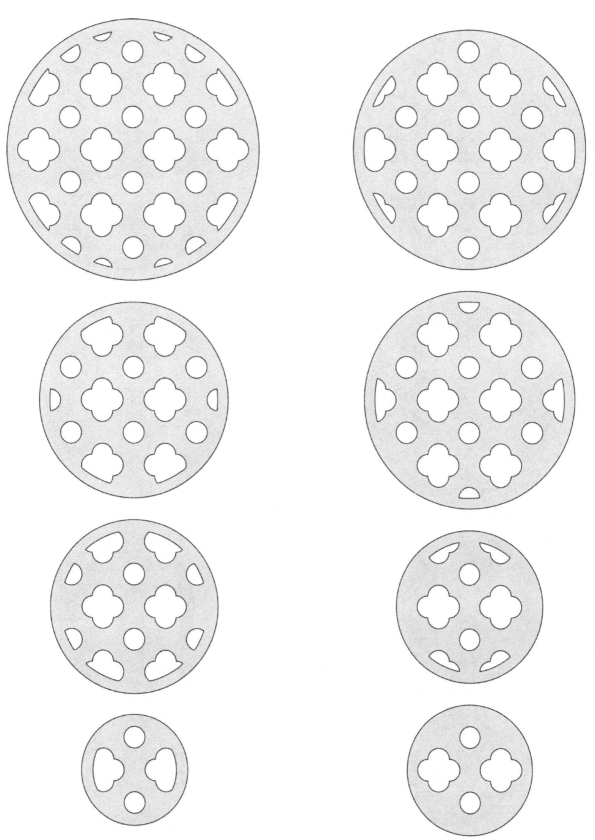

128

129

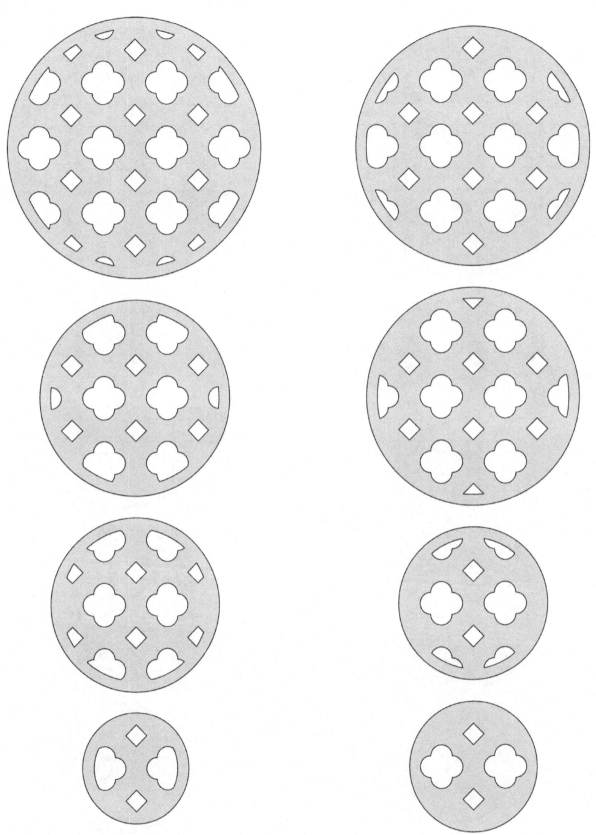

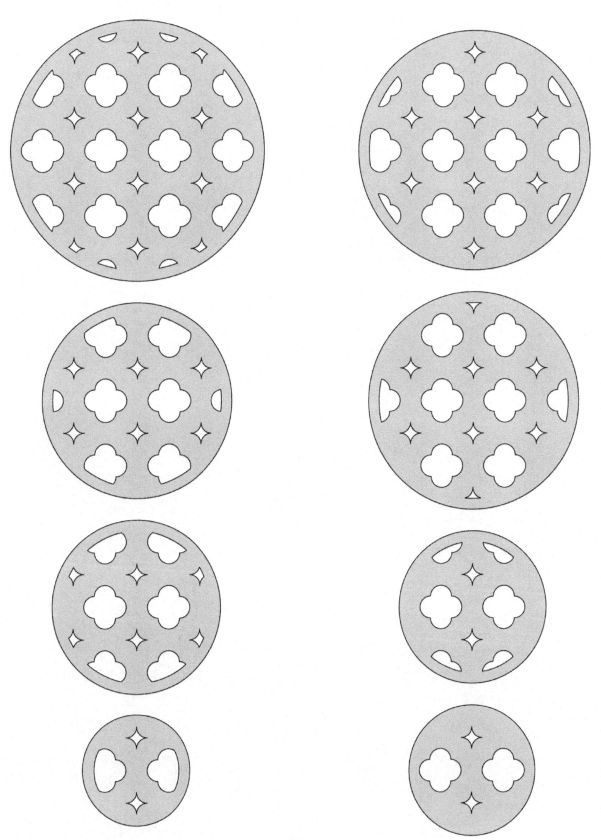

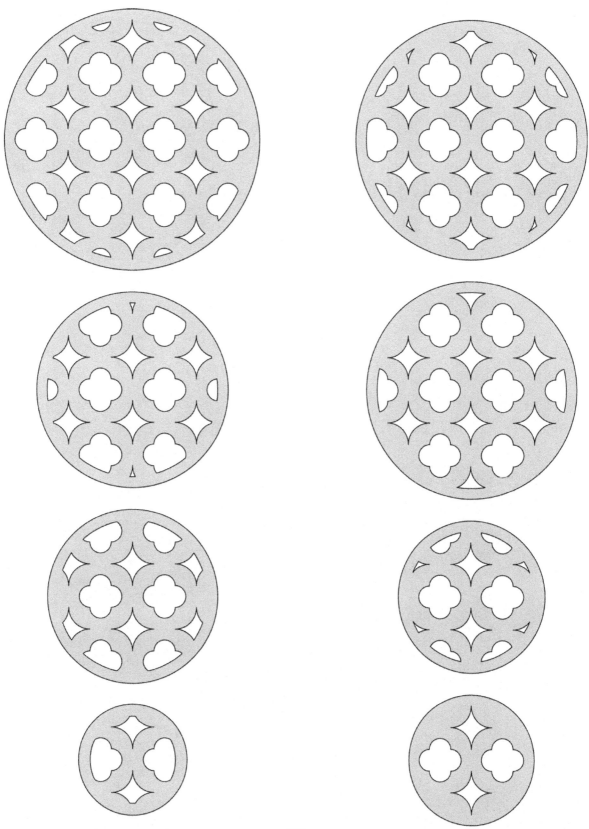

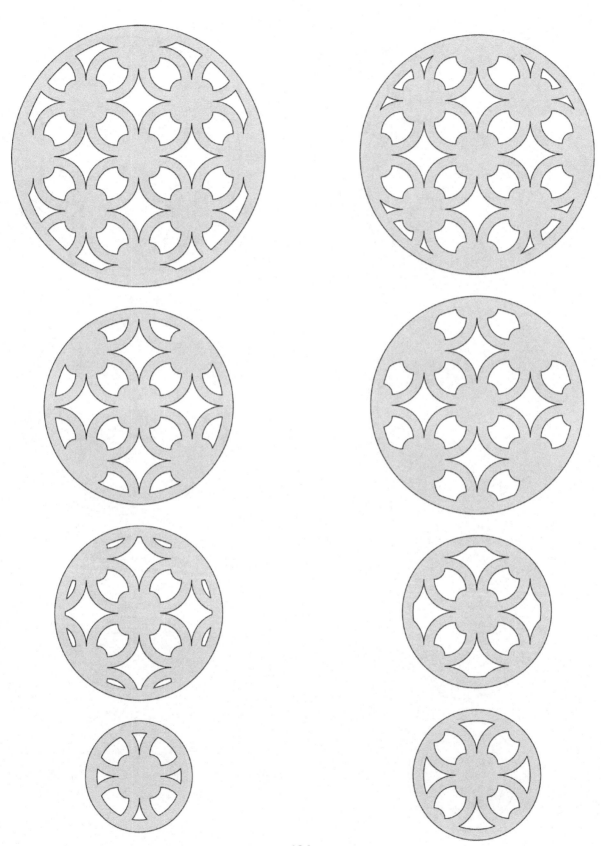

137

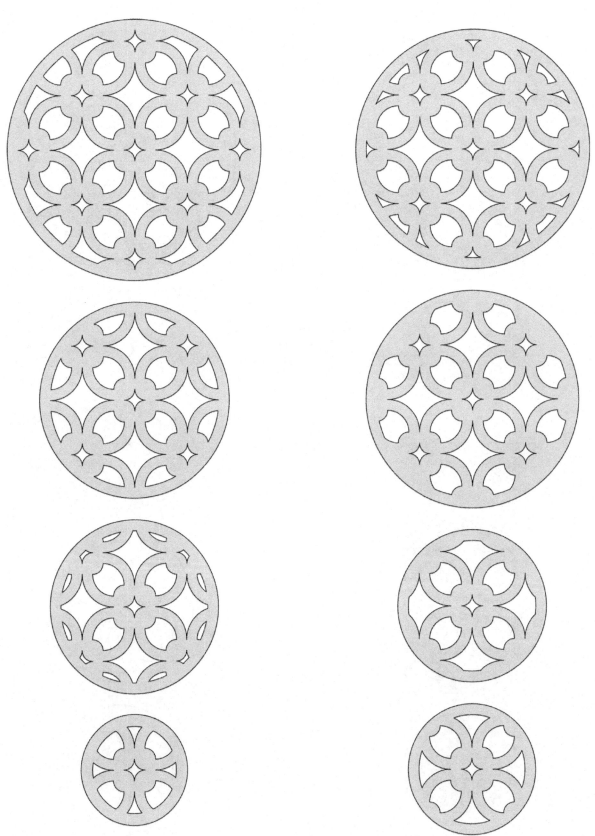

138

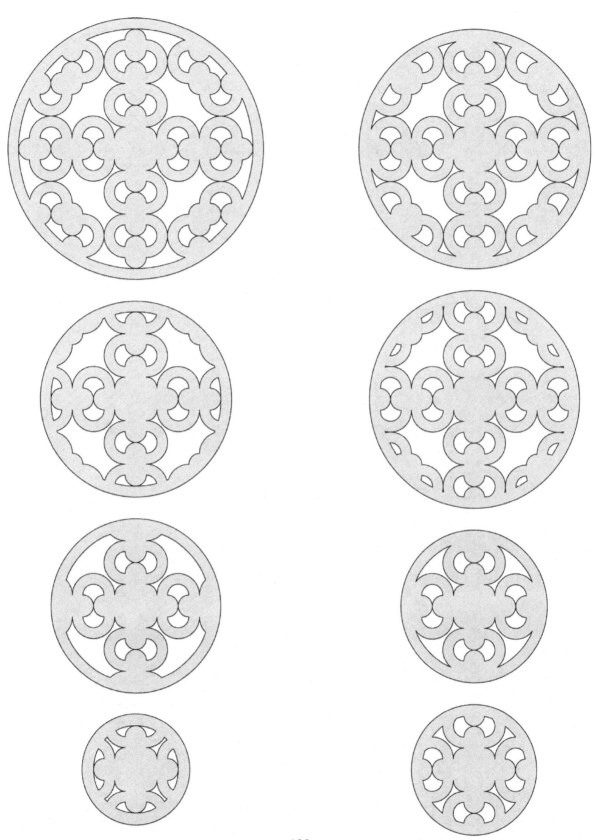

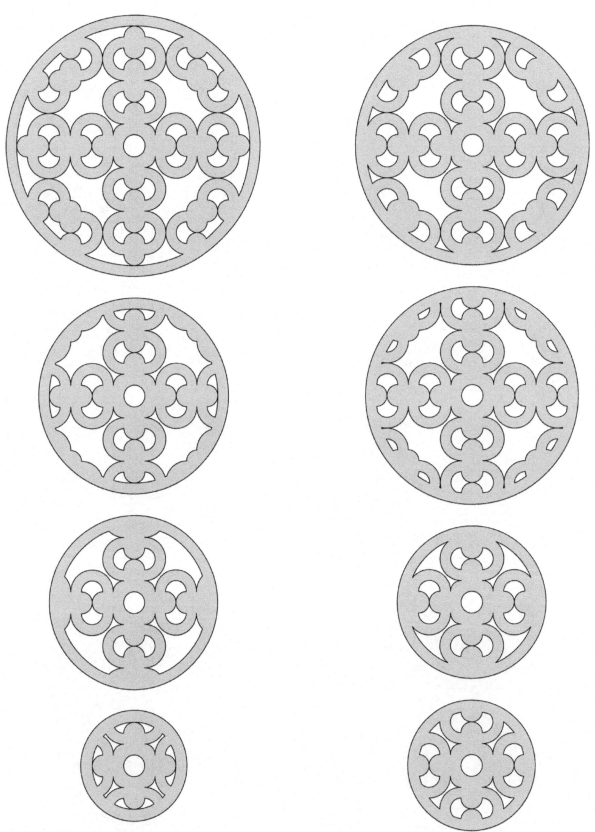

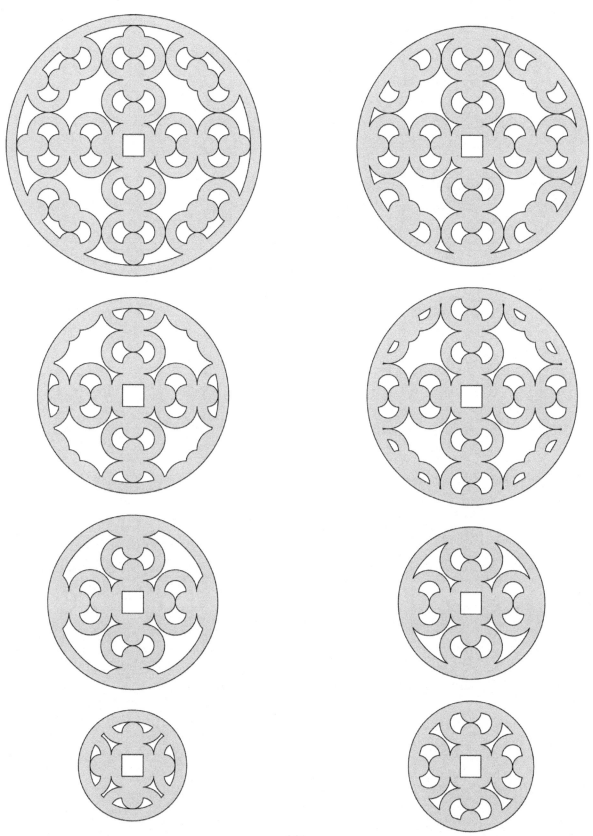

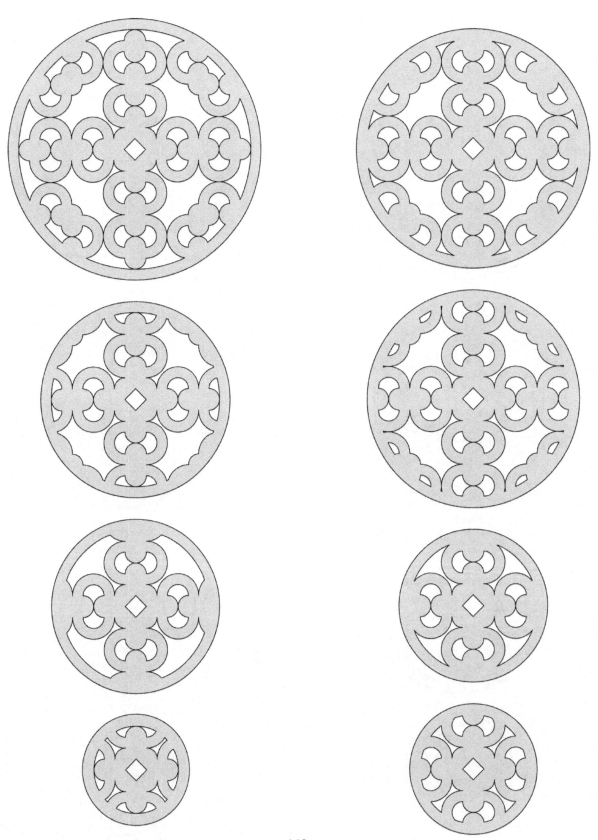

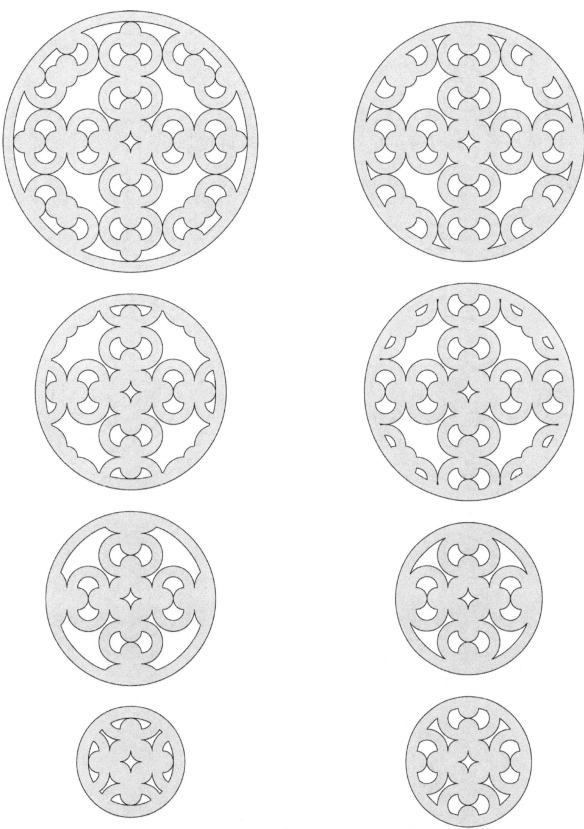

151

157

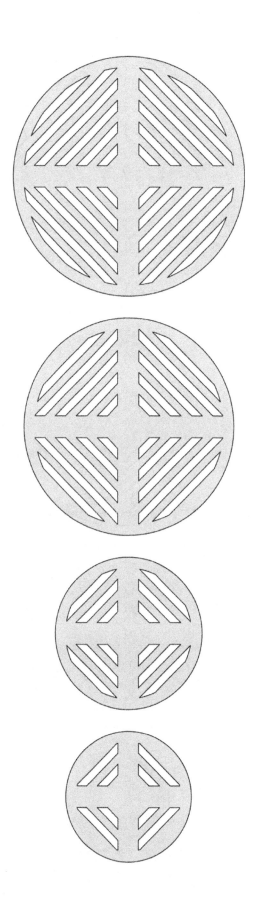

160

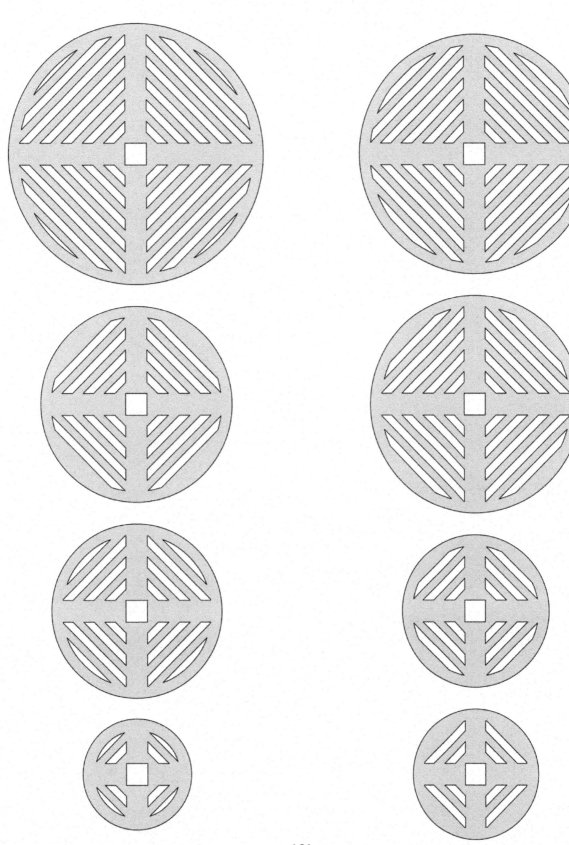

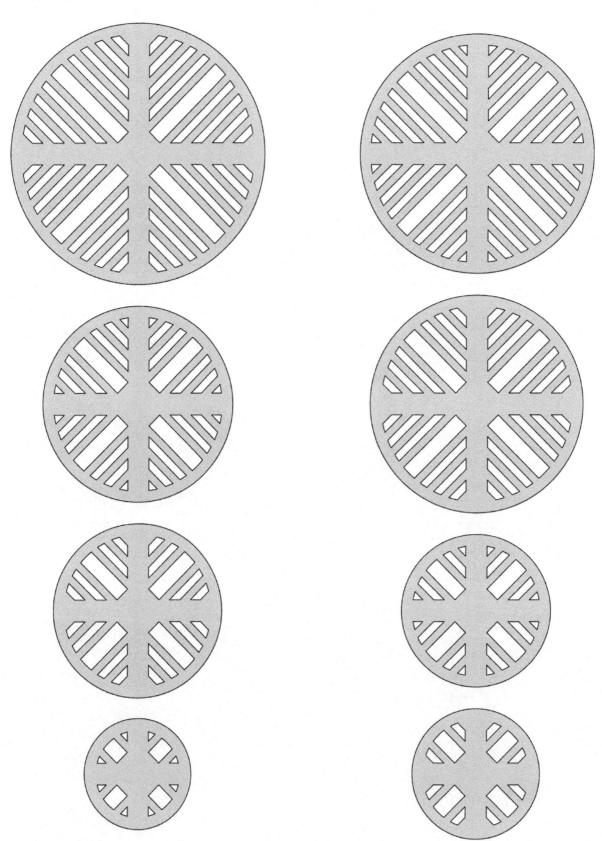

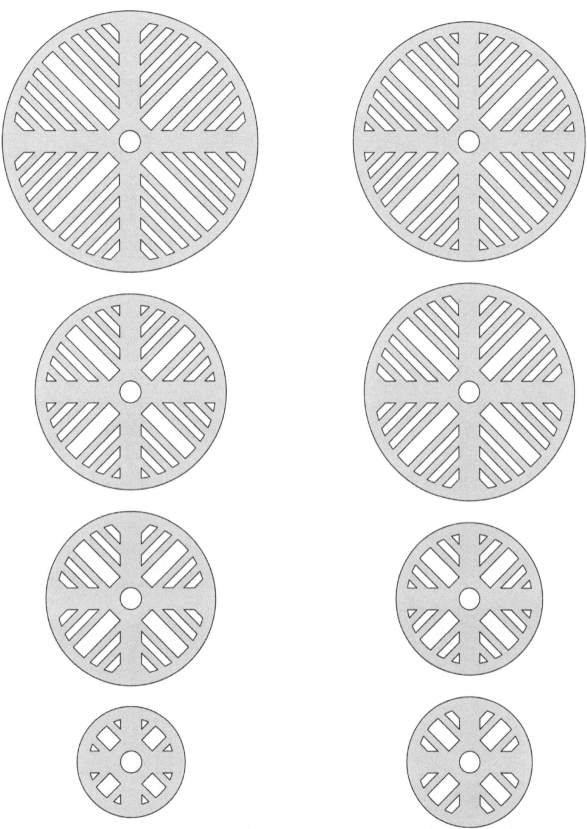

165

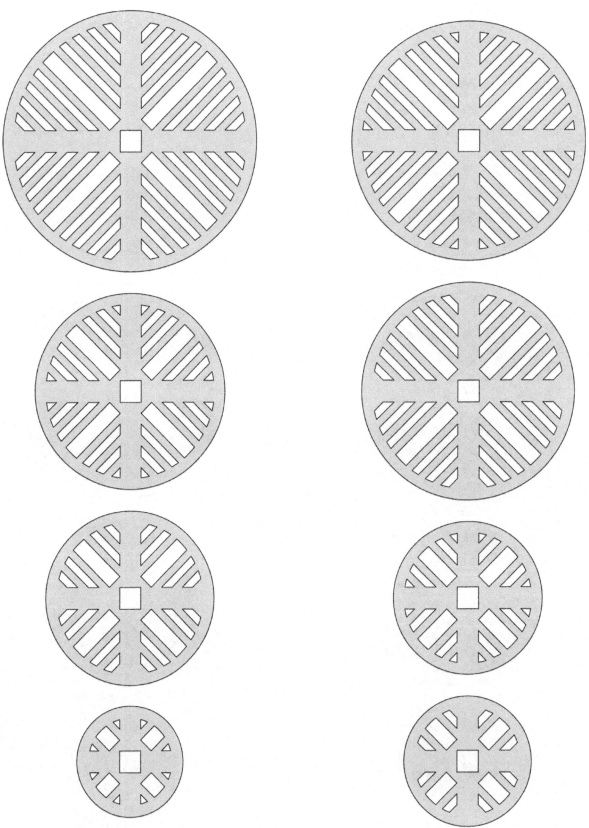

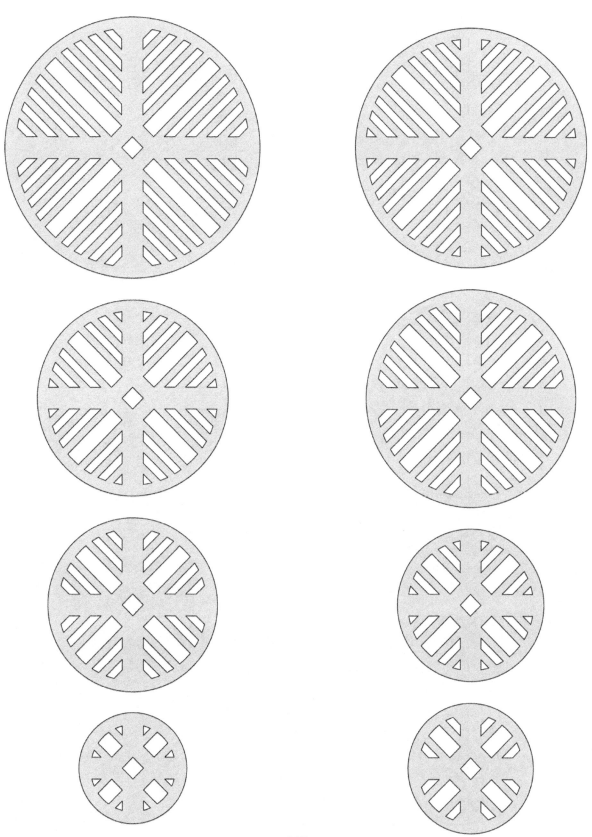

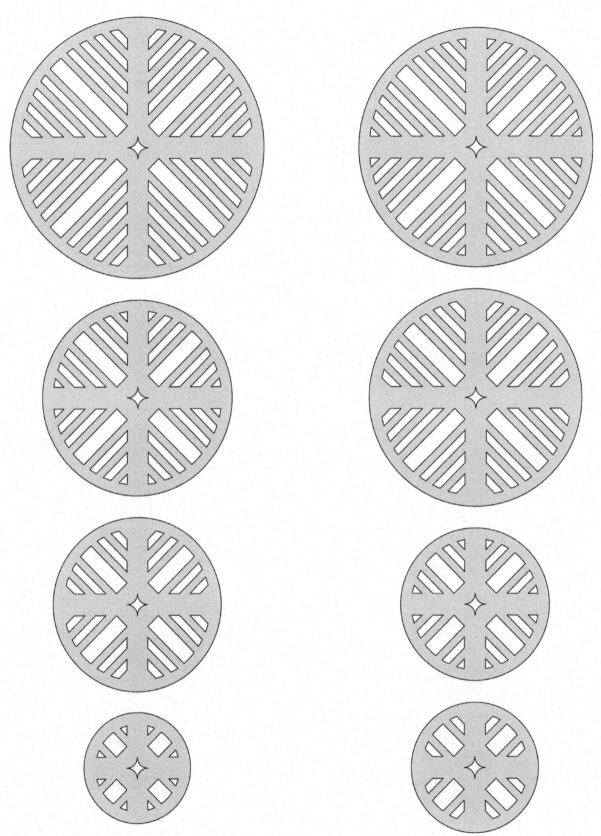

CPSIA information can be obtained at www.ICGtesting.com
Printed in the USA
LVOW03s1919010415

432906LV00002B/64/P